Remember ... it's for Ireland

A FAMILY MEMOIR OF TOMÁS Mac CURTÁIN

> My fore fathers and yours thank God — stood for Ireland and were hunted some of them from their homes for their fidelity, we are to-day proud of their sacrifices and honour their memory,

WRITTEN BY TOMÁS TO EILÍS
24 MAY 1917

*This book is dedicated to
my forefathers and the cause
they cherished and served
— Irish freedom*

Ní bheidh a leithéidí ann arís

Remember ... it's for Ireland

A FAMILY MEMOIR OF TOMÁS Mac CURTÁIN

FIONNUALA Mac CURTAIN

40 TOMAS MAC CURTAIN. 40

40

Cionssal na n-Artánac
ARTAN CLOTHING FACTORY

Contents

Eilís

'... Everything went against

me, except for two things

I had God, and I had you ...'

TRANSLATED EXTRACT FROM A POEM 'EILÍS' WRITTEN BY TOMÁS, 1916

Acknowledgements

My sincere thanks to my sister Orla, her husband Dessie and their boys for making New York my second home. I hope she is proud of my attempt to do justice to the lives of a remarkable couple, whom we were fortunate to have as our grandparents.

Orla, I and our brother Tomás, until his untimely death, were very lucky children. We were brought up basking in the love and approval of our parents. Mum is a very special woman. I can well understand why my father loved her. It takes an exceptional woman to stand beside an exceptional man. My father and grandfather believed that they were blessed with the women with whom they fell in love. Each believed that they could not even strive to fulfil their dreams without the support of these women.

My children Aron, Sarah, Ross, Ava and Tomás deserve to be mentioned for their patience with my constant pounding of the computer keys and the research papers scattered – everywhere.

Thanks also to Gerry White for sharing with me the fount of knowledge that he has on Irish history and more especially the keen interest he has shown in the contribution Tomás Mac Curtáin and his compatriots made to the cause of Irish freedom.

I most sincerely wish to thank all the team at Mercier Press, especially Mary Feehan – patience and encouragement must be her middle names.

It should be remembered that the late Florence O'Donoghue spent a great deal of time and put extraordinary effort into recording the life and writing the first biography of Tomás Mac Curtáin. Without his attention to detail in my grandfather's biography valuable information would have been lost. I am truly grateful for his account of events.

A most sincere thanks to Brother Beausang at the North Monastery in Cork. His translations are the work of a true Irish scholar.

During the research and writing of this book I was delighted to make the acquaintance of Conál Creedon and to be involved in his wonderful production *The Burning of Cork*. He has contributed greatly to the revival of interest in the history of our city.

The Blackpool Historical society and Cork Public Museum made their collection of papers and photographs available – I appreciate the courtesy and assistance they extended to me.

Tomás

Introduction

I t is only by looking back and honouring those who have gone before us that we can learn and move forward. Many comrades of both my grandfather and my father gave their lives, or spent their lifetimes striving, for a free Ireland. Their names will never appear in print. We should never forget the contribution made by others to get us to this point in the history of our island. It is because of the actions of these men and women we now stand equal to other nations.

Although this is not a history book, it has been essential to list people, organisations and places that had a direct impact on the lives of the Mac Curtáin family. I have only provided scant details of many important people and events that took place in Irish history in the 1900s. I felt that further historical information would detract from the story that I wished to tell. I would suggest reading *Baptised in Blood, Rebel Cork's Fighting Story* and of course Florence O'Donoghue's biography on my grandfather for further historical insight into the years 1915–1920.

The horrific circumstances of my grandfather's murder eclipsed his life. Recalling him, a shadow of sorrow passes over those reminiscing. A sense of sadness and horror still tinges the conversation.

It has been that way for as long as I can remember. I hope to adjust the balance in some small measure.

Having read this personal account of my grandparents' lives I hope that readers, when hearing the name Tomás Mac Curtáin, will smile and think a little of the poet, musician and family man and hold a picture in their mind of a sincere proud soldier of the Irish Volunteers, wearing the mayoral chain of his beloved Cork City, his Fáinne glistening on his lapel. Though his life was cut brutally short, he was a remarkable man who left a legacy that should be treasured. We are only minding it for our children.

This is my account of my grandparents who lived through turbulent times. Tomás and Elizabeth were a very religious couple with a deep love of this nation, its traditions and culture. Their story illustrates the belief that underpinned their lives: that it was worth fighting and dying for the freedom of Ireland. Both believed that unless they entered the armed struggle, freedom would never be attained. Self-determination certainly was not something that the British government held the power to bestow upon the Irish people – it was a basic right. Hopefully, their dream will become a reality without further bloodshed.

The generations who have gone before me acted on, and certainly suffered for, the principles they held so dear. My grandfather paid what many would consider the ultimate price – he gave his life.

My father also paid a very high price. He lived his life true to his unwavering principles. He has, I believe, yet to be fully recognised for his contribution to the cause of Irish freedom. I am so proud that he was my father.

The Mac Curtáin name belonged to people who would not compromise their principles. They knew the true meaning of the words 'honour' and 'principle'. I am extremely fortunate that my relatives preserved many personal letters and archive material. Their memories, reflections and their power of story-telling provided me with invaluable assistance. The love Tomás and Eilís Mac Curtáin had for their country and their city was unquestionably passed on to their children.

The love they had for each other shone through at all times and gave my grandmother the strength to carry on her life and devote her time to her children and to the cause of Irish freedom.

You will notice the various different spellings of the Mac Curtain name. Tomás used the Irish version [Mac Curtáin] but his extended family used Mac Curtain.

Fionnuala Mac Curtain

1

Remember ... it's for Ireland

Whispers of 'the Lord Mayor is dead' spread over the city of Cork like a fog sweeping in from the sea. What began as a rumour at about 2 a.m. became a confirmed fact as the morning dawned.

Scant details emerged – masked, armed men had broken into the Lord Mayor's home at approximately 1.15 a.m., pushed his pregnant wife out of the way and shot him at his bedroom door. The gun was discharged at point blank range. His wife and young children witnessed the scene.

The city became engulfed in grief and disbelief. An almost audible silence descended on Cork. Mac Curtáin had held the Mayoral office for only fifty days.

The incredulous fact was confirmed; Tomás Mac Curtáin, the

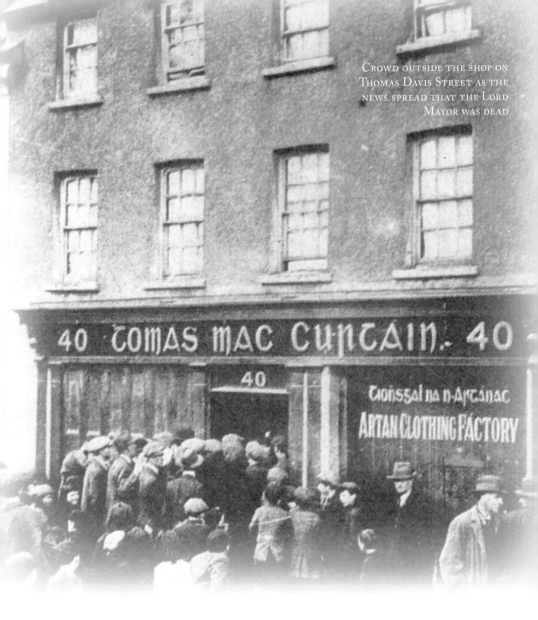

first Republican Lord Mayor of Cork, was dead. An outrageous act of murder had taken place in the city.

His last words were, 'Into thy hands O Lord I commend my spirit'. His wife Elizabeth watched as her husband took his last breath and whispered to him, 'Remember darling, it's all for Ireland'.

The morning of his thirty-sixth birthday had dawned. Tomás' surprise birthday party would now become his wake.

Tomás

One of the official pictures taken on the night Tomás was elected Lord Mayor

Elizabeth Walsh

Mother

Hannah Johnson-Gunn

Father

John Walsh

Children

Annie	Mary
Hannah	Sue
Elizabeth	Thomas
James	

Tomás Mac Curtáin

Mother

Julia Sheehan

Father

Patrick Curtin

Children

Patrick	Hannorah & Michael (twins)
Margaret	Owen
Ellen	Eugene
Julia	Michael
Mary	John
(Thomas) Tomás	

Children of Tomás & Eilís

Siobhán	Tomás
Síle	Máire
Patrick (died of Meningitis, 1914)	Eilís

2

Strong Roots

It seemed to all in the district that Patrick Curtin had done well for himself when he married Julia Sheehan. Her brother and father had died and she was in real danger of losing the tenancy for the farm that was part of the holding of their landlord, a protestant named Ware. Land and holdings were very important. In a way, they showed who you were and your standing in society. Both of them understood this.

She was only seventeen at the time and had no hope of securing the property herself. In truth, she could not have faced the struggle to survive on her own. Life had been difficult since the death of her mother and she was broken-hearted at the loss of what had been left of her small family – now it was almost unbearable. The parish priest had arranged the first meeting with Pat. Things, you would say, went from strength to strength between them – they were very attracted to each other and fell in love.

The marriage meant that Pat moved from his family home at Kilavullen and set up home with Julia at Ballyknockane, Mourneabbey. Their farm was close to the milestone that told a passer-by that he had fourteen miles left on the journey into Cork city.

Julia was an unusual child. Her father Michael had worked on the farm but also taught at the local hedge school, as did Patrick's relations. Julia learned a lot from him and in turn passed on to her children her love of Irish culture and language. Both she and Pat were fluent Irish speakers.

It was a very happy and busy household. They had a large family. Tom, like his siblings, was born at Bally-knockane and entered the world on 20 March 1884 to join the family then known as the Curtins. Tommy as he was affectionately called as a baby, was the youngest of twelve children and was spoilt and indulged by all from birth. He inherited the passion to learn and a deep love of the Irish language – this love encompassed Irish culture – and the development of Ireland as a nation fascinated him. Nobody thought this was strange, as all the family naturally embraced the interests of their parents and the passion that drove them to make sure that the Irish lifestyle and traditions would not just survive, but grow and flourish.

At the age of thirteen, Tom had outgrown Burnfort School.

> As he grew up Tom inherited the passion to learn and a deep love of the Irish language – this love encompassed Irish culture – and the development of Ireland as a nation fascinated him.

Breitheanna a Cláraíodh i gCeantar / Births Registered in the District of _Kilshannig_ i gC / in th

Uimh.	Dáta agus Ionad Breithe	Ainm (má tugadh)	Gnéas	Ainm, Sloinne agus Ionad Chónaithe an Athar
No. (1)	Date and Place of Birth (2)	Name (if any) (3)	Sex (4)	Name and Surname and Dwelling Place of Father (5)
H36.	1884. Twentieth March Ballyknockan	Thomas	Male.	Patrick Curtin Ballyknockan

Many of his classmates were going out to work but he had the opportunity of keeping up his studies by moving into the city of Cork and going to live with his sister Mary, known as Minnie. Minnie and Bill Twomey had no children and welcomed Tom with open arms.

Their house at 68 Great Britain Street became his home from home. This made it possible for him to go to the North Monastery secondary school, and this change in his lifestyle was in many ways the turning point of his life. He became immersed in his studies and became close friends with an older student, Terence MacSwiney.

Although these students were very different and there was a five-year age gap between them, they became best friends and

IRELAND

hun na hAchta um Chlárú Breitheanna agus Básanna 1863 go 1972.

nce of Births and Deaths Registration Acts 1863 to 1972.

an Chláraitheora Maoirseachta do rintendent Registrar's District of	Mallow		i gContae in the County

Ainm agus Sloinne na Máthar agus a Sloinne roimh Phósadh di / Name and Surname and Maiden Surname of Mother (6)	Céim nó Gairm Bheatha an Athar / Rank or Profession of Father (7)	Siniú, Cáiliocht agus Ionad Chónaithe an Fháisnéiseora / Signature, Qualification and Residence of Informant (8)	An Dáta a Cláraíodh / When Registered (9)
Julia Curtin / Iníon Formerly / Sheehan .	Farmer	Her / Mary x Curtin / Mark . / Present at birth. / Ballyknockan .	Twenty Third apal 1884 .

BIRTH CERTIFICATE OF THOMAS CURTIN, LATER KNOWN AS TOMÁS MAC CURTÁIN

their short lives were to run on parallel tracks for approximately twenty years. Their friendship endured everything that life could throw at them and later, even in death, they would be forever remembered with the one breath. They left an indelible mark not only on the history of Cork and Ireland, but also on the world stage.

3

The Early Years

Learning was never a hardship to Tom and at the North Monastery he soaked up knowledge. He had an unquenchable thirst for any information on Ireland. He devoured books on history or the Irish language and sought more. As a student he had an infectious enthusiasm for everything and was rapidly making a name for himself. Even at this early stage, a youth of barely eighteen years old, he had been identified as somebody exceptional. He excelled in many subjects but when it came to Irish and history he was as well read as many of his teachers. He was totally at ease mixing with his elders – probably because he was the youngest of such a large family.

There are milestones in people's lives, dates or years that stand out. For Tom Curtin a new start came when a friend, Con Collins, brought him to a Gaelic League meeting in Blackpool. Douglas Hyde, Eoin MacNeill and Eugene O'Growney founded the Gaelic League (Conradh na Gaeilge) in 1893 to ensure that the Irish language would be spoken in Ireland. Part of the fall out of the famine seemed to be that the Irish language was put into second place and the English language came across as a symbol of prosperity and progress – and it was the language of the national school system. Blackpool was a fledgling branch and was crying out for volunteer workers. It was an outlet for Tom and he enjoyed going to the branch with people, of both sexes and all occupations, who shared his love for the Irish culture.

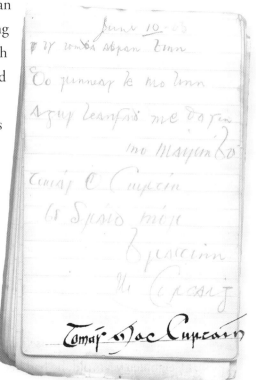

Tom's music, and especially his violin, was his source of recreation. One of his favourite tunes was 'The Lark in the Clear Air' and this melody could be heard at any time day or night when the notion took him to play. He loved attending the Feis and playing in the Blackpool orchestra, of which he was a founder member. When Tomás became secretary of his branch of the League in 1902, he persuaded Professor George Brady to conduct this local orchestra.

It was around this time that he began using the Irish version of his name. He tried out many variations but with the influence of the brothers at the monastery, he decided on Tomás Mac Curtáin as being the correct translation of Tom Curtin and used the Irish version of his name from then on.

Tomás' first gainful employment was with the City of Cork

Steam Packet Company. The anticipation of a pay packet was exciting and there was a great sense of achievement for the first-time 'earner'. In his spare time, he was teaching and helping with the Gaelic League and the association had gone from strength to strength since Rev. Austin Quigley, the prior of St Mary's, had taken over as its president.

Mac Curtáin was torn in two. Work was essential to live but teaching was his life, and knowledge was definitely the food of his soul and mind. He believed an employer deserved a full and honest day's work. On the other hand, he was only waiting to finish his job to go and study, teach or play music.

Blackpool orchestra

Fionán Mc Colum, of the Gaelic League, spotted his talents and stamina – not only his ability to speak and teach Irish but also his extraordinary communication skills and his natural ability to organise. He was systematic and methodical about everything he did. Every undertaking was seen to its conclusion and he always strove for improvement. He set himself personal goals and as he came near to accomplishing them, he raised the bar higher. Tomás possessed an uncanny gift of being able to match the right man to the right job and he commanded respect. He was a gifted strategist and a valuable asset to any organisation as he was a born leader and people automatically gravitated towards him.

ADVERT ISSUED BY THE CITY OF CORK STEAM PACKET COMPANY

Fionán was swamped with work. He was teaching and organising the League all over Munster and was crying out for help. He was looking around for somebody with enthusiasm that would match his own. Boundless energy was the other necessary attribute. It was not long before he approached Tomás to give up his position of clerk and throw himself totally into the work of the League. Tomás went around with a grin on his face that could not be wiped off. He felt as if all his birthdays had come together. What a job! It was made in heaven for him.

The amount of time and energy he channelled into his new full-time career was incredible. He covered rural and urban areas that could have been the territory of three men. Month after month, he travelled the length and breadth of not just the county but also nearly the whole south of Ireland and was welcomed with open arms by families and societies. He made infrequent trips back to Cork, but never lingered more than a day or two before setting off again. His sister and family never saw much of him and when he was around, he was to be found immersed in paper work.

By late 1906 Tomás was ready to return to Cork as his mind and body were exhausted from the amount of travelling he was doing and he longed for some time to be able to stop, think and re-evaluate where the movement was and what further structures were needed to go forward. He would have welcomed the opportunity of some further personal studies but knew that was not going to happen in the near future. He needed a job back in the city and eventually got work at Mack's Mills.

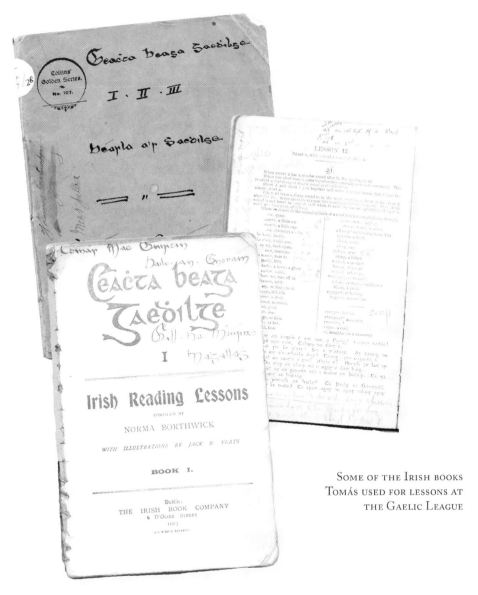

SOME OF THE IRISH BOOKS
TOMÁS USED FOR LESSONS AT
THE GAELIC LEAGUE

One of the few consistencies in his life was his family and his friends in the Blackpool branch of the League. They gave him a sense of grounding, a reminder of his roots. It was on one of his visits to the League that Tomás met Elizabeth Walsh. The regular teacher was ill and Tomás was asked to stand in at the last moment and instruct the class. Fate worked its magic and Elizabeth came along to the class with her friends. He was attracted to her from the beginning but thought that their relationship could never come to anything. He was on the road all the time and lacked financial stability. More importantly, he was totally committed to making sure that Ireland held, and improved, her identity as a nation. Around the same time, he joined Sinn Féin. Since the early 1900s, this was the only organisation publicly declaring the idea of a free nation. Its views were the closest to Tomás' own opinions.

He knew that having a serious relationship with Elizabeth would make it very difficult for her, in fact for any woman, as she would have to accept second place in his life. This did not prevent him from becoming utterly besotted with her. Lizzie, as she was affectionately known, was five foot eight inches tall and had a strong personality. She was born close to the Mardyke and her mother was one of the Johnson-Gunns, Scottish Presbyterians who had originally lived in Bandon, County Cork. Her father's side of the family were strong Fenians and some of his family had fled Ireland and joined the wagon trail to Oregon in the 1800s. The family had lost track of them in America but news came back after many years that an Apache tribe had attacked them and there was no word of any survivors.

Her sisters Susie and Annie were teachers and from a young age exhibited symptoms of wanderlust. Unusual as it was for women

I remember, my love, the very first time we met
At the Blackpool branch of the Gaelic League;
You sent my heart racing, Eilís Walsh,
Filling it with your love.
I was so moved by your sweet little mouth,
And your slim body, as you held your camogie stick
I would have given everything just then
For you to speak to me.
In the lovely month of August you came to me
Inside Teach Éireann, I will remember it forever,
My secret love, in that small pleasant
Classroom at Pine Street

TRANSLATION OF AN EXCERPT FROM A POEM
TOMÁS WROTE ABOUT EILÍS

of their time, they wanted to see the world – explore other cultures and travel.

Elizabeth fancied the teacher at the League. Some of the girls were talking about their fellow students and Elizabeth said that they should be looking at the teacher. She regretted that as soon as she had said it – there could be strong competition for his attention!

One night after a League session, Tomás and Elizabeth were talking about Cork and the river Lee when she told him, 'I drank

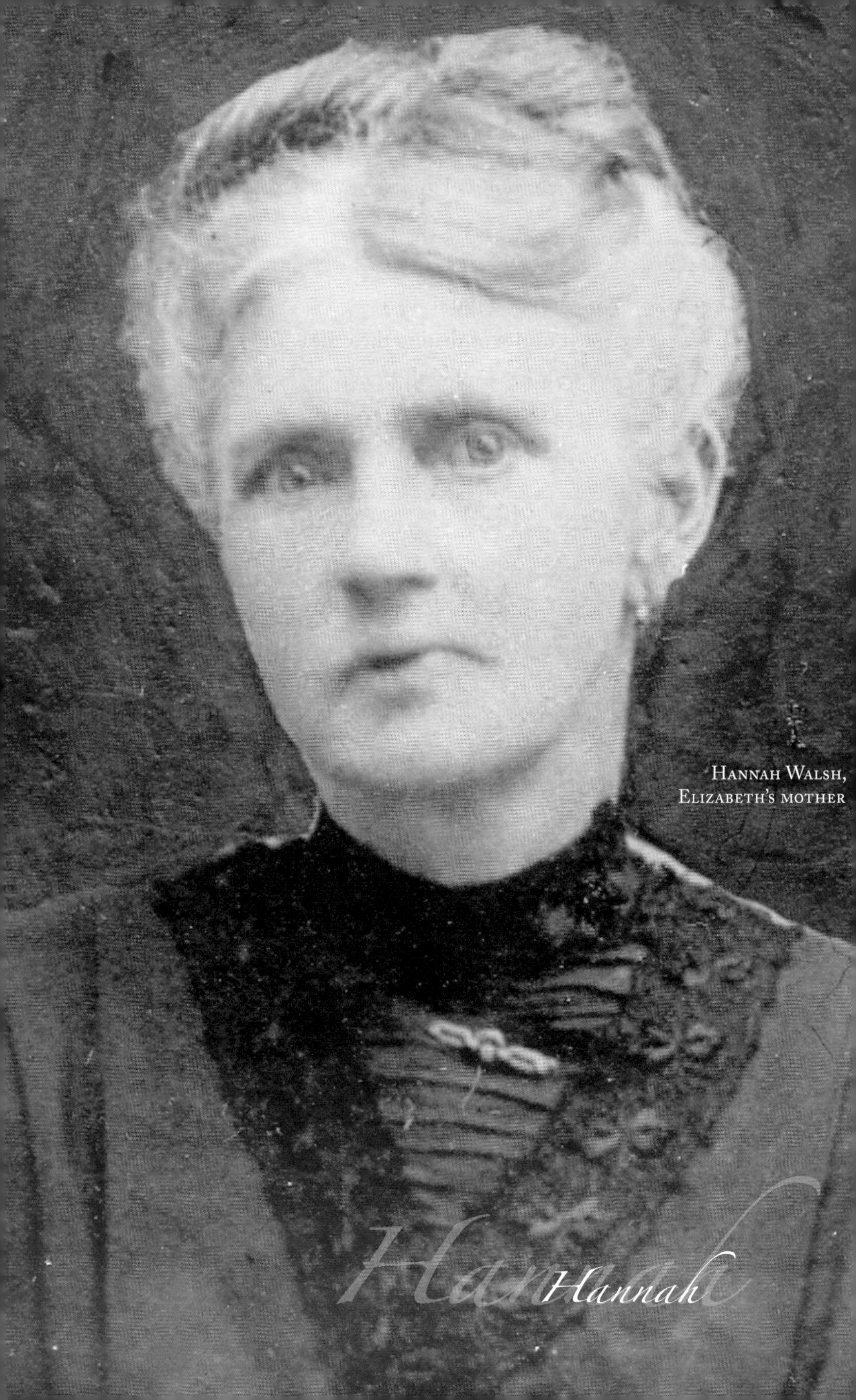

Hannah Walsh,
Elizabeth's mother

its waters with my mother's milk. How else can I account for the grip it has on me?

'It appears a meandering river to those who do not come from Cork. To us it is a stream of liquid history.'

They never seemed to tire of sharing their ideas and Elizabeth often surprised him with her profound thoughts. They both had a passion for the countryside and more especially Cork and the outlying area. One night she looked far away and pensive. He asked her, 'Elizabeth dear, what are you thinking of?'

'There is no doubt that we resemble our natural surroundings,' she said. 'The Connemara man is big, bony and self-sufficient, dignified and quiet, taking his big stature from the limey soil and his quiet austere manner from the example of nature around him.

'The Kerry man, squat with his long thoughts beneath his deep-set eyes and low brow. The black bleak mountains are his background, the poor soil. He is sturdy and strong so that he may defy the hardy blast from the Atlantic on his shores.

> It appears a meandering river to those who do not come from Cork. To us it is a stream of liquid history.

'And there is the Cork man who resembles nature in his virtue and his faults. The gushing, noisy, lazy, wide, lavish river. The stubborn hesitant coquettish stream, that goes on to form our river Lee. She has her source near Gougane, near Finbarr's island, flows through Ballingeary and along by Inchigeela. There she reaches adolescence, then past Macroom and into Inniscarra where she is at the peak of her beauty. Here ... her banks are lined with heather and green ferns galore, while green fields mark her boundary and big salmon are here by the hundred. She becomes ... full flown and spreads out over the land. At the Lee Fields, age creeps on her then and she gathers herself in again and flows quietly through the city like a sedate matron or a distant swan until she finds her way to the sea'.

Tomás listening with a twinkle in his eye, smoking his pipe, was obviously enjoying their time together.

He courted Elizabeth for some time. He knew very well that being young and poor he could not offer her much in the line of security. There was not going to be any change in his circumstances in the near future. In his favour, he loved her very much and to onlookers they were a perfect couple.

One late autumn day in 1906, he took her for a walk along the Mardyke, on a tree-lined pathway used by young and old alike. At any time of day there were always people strolling along this path, some arm in arm, some deep in conversation and others on their own, thinking their own thoughts and soaking in the peace and tranquillity of the area.

It took him a while to come to the point, and even then it was an indirect approach. Standing under the third tree he said, 'I know a fellow in our office who is getting married on £2 a week. Hasn't he a nerve asking a girl to marry him on that?'

Elizabeth, who was more or less expecting this, answered that she thought a girl might manage on it. Anyway, the result of all this talk was that they came out from under that tree promised to each other.

Tomás made sure that Elizabeth was fully aware of his commitment to the cause of Irish freedom. In 1907 he joined the IRB, whose aim was to gain Irish freedom, and by resorting to force if

John Walsh,
Elizabeth's father

John

necessary. This was not a surprise to Elizabeth as they had talked about their desire for Irish freedom and the path ahead was clear for them. He wanted to make sure that his marriage would be on a solid footing; Lizzie knew the contribution he had made to the various organisations and was very proud of him. She believed that the public had only seen the tip of the iceberg when it came to Tomás' talents and there was far more to this man than anybody else had seen – yet. He had found an eager ally in Elizabeth.

The 28 June 1908 dawned bright and the household at Prospect Row was buzzing with excitement. Surrounded by family and friends Tomás married Elizabeth in St Peter and Paul's church. The ceremony was followed by a small wedding breakfast and then Tomás had to return to his job. He had just about managed to get a half-day from work.

> They set out on their life together fully aware that the path ahead would be strewn with difficulties ...

They set out on their life together fully aware that the path ahead would be strewn with difficulties; not from any friction within their marriage but from what the outside world would throw at them.

Their new house, near the Mardyke, was in a beautiful part of the city. It was with an air of excitement they set up home a short walk from the third tree in the row along the walkway. Elizabeth would always smile when they passed it – and remember their special afternoon.

It was during this time that Tomás became more focused on

ÉIRE   IRELAND

Cóip deimhnithe de Thaifid i gClár Leabhar Póstaí.
Certified Copy of Entry in the Marriage Register Book.

Pósadh a Sollúnaíodh i solemnised at the Catholic _Chruch_ de of SS. _Peter & Paul_ i gCeantar an Chláraitheora do in the Registrar's District of _No. 4 Urban_								
i gCeantar an Chláraitheora Maoirseachta do in the Superintendent Registrar's District of _Cork_					i gContae in the County of _Cork_		Éire Ireland.	
...ta an Phósta ...hen Married. 2.	Ainm agus Sloinne Name and Surname. 3.	Aois Age. 4.	Staid Condition. 5.	Slí Bheatha Rank or Profession. 6.	Ionad Chónaithe Residence at the time of Marriage. 7.	Ainm agus Sloinne an Athar Father's Name and Surname. 8.	Slí Bheatha an Athar Rank or Profession of Father. 9.	
June 25th 1908	Thomas Curtin	full	Bachelor	clerk	68 Wm. O'Brien St.,	Patrick Curtin	farmer	
	Elizabeth Walsh	full	Spinster		6 Prospect Row (off Henry St.,)	John Walsh	mason	

...c Roman Catholic _Church_ of _SS. Peter & Paul_ de réir Uird agus Deasghnath na h-Eaglaise Caitlicí agamsa according to the Rites and Ceremonies of the Catholic Church by me _Patrick A. Locke_

Tomás Mac Curtáin (Thomas Curtin) In la Láthair _Seaghán Mac Curtin (...)_

MARRIAGE CERTIFICATE OF EILÍS AND TOMÁS. SURROUNDED BY FAMILY AND FRIENDS,
TOMÁS MARRIED ELIZABETH IN ST PETER AND PAUL'S CHURCH

action. He had always thought that Ireland was too dependent on England. He believed that Ireland, as a nation, was developing under the influence of the British empire, rather than as a small nation with its own culture, taking its rightful place in the world. It was difficult as England was the nearest landmass for exports, but the problem was deeper than this. The English language was the spoken word and British culture was creeping in. He felt people would have to be made more aware of their heritage or they would lose their identity as Irish individuals and as a nation.

His commitment to the possibility of action was not taken easily. Tomás had studied the course of Irish history and had learned that the British government had never kept its word where Ireland was concerned. The British establishment treated Ireland as a poor relation and as an island off the mainland. The failed rising of the IRB in the 1860s had diluted its numbers to just the hard-core believers. Many of its leaders were exiled, but the remaining few had kept it going. With the turn of the century came the need to recruit new blood, fresh ideas and men of action, and who better than Tomás Mac Curtáin in Cork? These new men with ideas of freedom found willing ears to listen to them. Tomás threw himself wholeheartedly into any movement that propelled the idea of a cultural revival forward. A free nation was more than an aspiration – it was his goal.

A branch of Fianna Éireann started in 1911 and Tomás not only joined but also became treasurer. There were obvious difficulties as he was now a member of many different organisations and was juggling his time between home, work and the commitments he had made to the various groups of which he was a member. Early in 1912, he was offered a position as a clerk in Suttons and as the salary was better he and Elizabeth decided that he should make the change.

With his colleagues in the League he watched the development of the changing relationship between England and Ireland. When the Third Home Rule Bill was introduced in late summer 1912, it sparked a crisis in Ireland and it was generally assumed that the bill would become law within two years.

4

Broken Hearts

⟨⎯⎯

The possibility of the implementation of Home Rule brought objections from Edward Carson's followers and members of the Ulster Volunteer Force [UVF] in the north-east. A reaction was bound to follow from the nationalists, many of whom were in the IRB and Gaelic League in the south. Tomás came home with the news that Bulmer Hobson and The O'Rahilly, members of the Gaelic League, spoke about forming a Volunteer force. This idea grew, support was gained and by the end of November of that year, a bulletin was sent around the country advising all interested parties of the formation of the Irish Volunteers. The public meeting, on 25 November 1913 in Dublin, was over-run with people eager to hear about this new group.

While all this was going on in the public arena, Tomás and Elizabeth had settled down to married life. They were delighted when they discovered that Elizabeth was pregnant and were overjoyed at the birth of a healthy baby girl. They decided to call her Siobhán – the Irish version of Suzanne – after Elizabeth's sister, known as Susie. Síle was born next and then a baby son, Patrick – named after Tomás' father. The house was a permanent hive of activity and Elizabeth thrived on motherhood.

Unexpectedly, like a bolt of lightning, sorrow fell on the household. Their only son, Patrick, aged three, a source of great pride and joy was struck down with an illness similar to meningitis and died on 25 November – the very same day as the Volunteer meeting was taking place in Dublin. Elizabeth thanked God Tomás had stayed at home.

Entry of baby Patrick's death in the city register

The next day was bleak and as the family walked from the gates of the cemetery to the grave their journey seemed to get longer with every step they took. Elizabeth and Tomás were brokenhearted. Their world had been turned upside down and life would never be the same again. It was so difficult to explain to his two young sisters that their baby brother was gone – that he would not be coming home again. Every time Siobhán or Síle asked for him, Elizabeth felt like a knife was turning in her heart

There was further grief when the baby that Elizabeth was carrying at this time was born just after Christmas. A perfect baby boy, full term but stillborn. The household reeled from the shock and all of them were plunged into the depths of sorrow. It had been a very difficult birth and Elizabeth struggled to get back on to her feet and to resume some semblance of normal life. In her heart, she felt things could never be normal again. For months, she went around doing what was necessary to keep the family home functioning but her heart was empty and she was completely drained.

Tomás never needed to find an excuse to work hard, but now he worked until he was exhausted as he hoped to block out some of his sorrow. It didn't work. Elizabeth's well-being was a constant worry to him even though she appeared to be coping well. In turn, she was worried about her husband. They both knew that the passage of time would help ease the pain, but in the meantime they had to cope with everyday life.

Their world had been turned upside down and life would never be the same again.

By now, many nationalists had heard of Pádraig Pearse in Dublin. Pearse's voice carried far, advocating the right to carry arms and defend one's nation. When the Volunteers were established, attention was focused on spreading the idea of freedom in the quickest possible time. By December 1913, the first meeting was held in Cork. J. J. Walsh, a comrade of Tomás, believed that the wave of enthusiasm for the new movement would be welcomed with open arms and embraced by all. Liam de Róiste was far more cautious and anticipated trouble and a very rocky path ahead of them.

Eoin MacNeill's first talk in mid December in City Hall, Cork ended in chaos. There were too many conflicting interests at the meeting and a riot ensued. The Hibernians did not like what was being said and confusion about the Ulster Volunteer movement fuelled the argument. The lights were turned off to give the impression that the meeting was over. The troublemakers eventually dispersed and the core of 'believers' bided their time. The lights were turned back on and the meeting quickly got down to business. Roger Casement assured the crowd that the way forward was to join the new Volunteer force.

It was Tomás' first meeting with Casement and he later told Elizabeth what happened that night and how impressed he was with Roger's contribution.

A committee was set up to start the administration of the Cork branch and to deal with the influx of new members. The provisional committee comprised chairman J. J. Walsh, with Diarmuid Fawsitt as vice-chairman, Tomás as the honorary secretary and Liam de Róiste as treasurer. The group all had very different and diverse interests but all had one aim in mind – they believed that it was worth fighting for the freedom of Ireland.

> The movement grew from strength to strength. By 1914, the Volunteers had become a force that was not going to disappear.

The movement grew from strength to strength. By 1914, the Volunteers had become a force that was not going to disappear. When John Redmond, leader of the Irish Parliamentary Party eventually accepted the movement, it was like the last piece of the jigsaw fell into place. His acceptance came at a price and the committee had to accept twenty-five Redmondite committee members. In Cork, Redmond's followers were co-opted onto the new committee to try to create harmony.

Tomás was juggling all this with work and his home life and there were never enough hours in the day.

He counted himself lucky to have Elizabeth and she acted like a personal secretary for him. The sorrows they had shared during the winter of 1913 had strengthened the bond that existed between them. All who encountered them or shared in their hospitality could not fail to see the love they shared.

> All who encountered them or shared in their hospitality could not fail to see the love that they shared.

5

Trouble in the Volunteers

The year 1914 had been rung in with much apprehension. The world was changing so fast. The broken-hearted couple had their surviving children, Siobhán age four and Síle age three, to mind. Elizabeth visited her family home at least twice a week to spend time with her mother. Her sisters Susie and Annie were travelling constantly and she liked to give her sister Hannah a break from looking after her elderly mother. Tomás and Elizabeth never lost their closeness as a couple and she considered him to be her best friend and was able to open up her heart and mind to him.

Tomás and Elizabeth were on the crest of the wave of emotions that was moving all organisations towards action. Elizabeth was very busy organising appointments, dealing with extremely confidential papers and overseeing private meetings in the house. Tomás was appointed to the military council of the Volunteers and this added to his ever-expanding list of duties. The areas were divided into companies which grew rapidly. The rural and urban areas were very different. Tomás paid particular attention to making sure that the rural units were not left out on the fringes. Blending them into one organisation and into a team of men that could work together, took thought and consideration. It took a lot of skill to achieve this and Tomás' attention to detail was critical.

> Tomás and Elizabeth were on the crest of the wave of emotions that was moving all organisations into action.

His work and relationship with local organisers was also important to the building of morale within the Volunteer movement. Uniforms were ordered and worn by those who could afford to buy them. Training marches took place, with hurleys and sticks instead of weapons. When some of the German firearms that were landed at Howth, known as the 'Howth rifles', made their way to Cork it was a huge boost to morale. It was not the number they received that was important, but the fact that they now had real guns.

War was now raging in Europe and Tomás and his comrades were watching with great interest. They were now part of a well-trained organisation in Ireland, though arms were limited. The British needed men to fight in France and Irishmen were joining the British army in droves. Tomás felt that they were needed at home to protect their own country and told Elizabeth that some of the Volunteers followed John Redmond, who advocated that Irishmen should serve in the British army and believed this was fair and just considering the circumstances of the war.

On 24 May 1914 a retired British army officer, Capt. Maurice Talbot Crosbie, joined the Volunteer movement enlisting in the Cork City Corps of Volunteers. He was so experienced that he was immediately elected commanding officer and exercised great influence over the men.

When war was declared, Talbot Crosbie said he wanted the Volunteers to offer their services to the crown and be supplied with arms. He announced this to the men while they were on parade and it came across to many Volunteers as the official view. Tomás was angry that he made this statement to the men as it was Talbot Crosbie's personal view. He felt he should not have made such a public statement without the consent of the committee. It was certainly not up to Talbot Crosbie to ask the men to volunteer or to apply to the British government for arms.

Crosbie would not be sidelined. He had made his statement and he was sticking to it. He wrote to the secretary of state offering the services of the Cork Corps. He read the reply, 'that their offer would be kept in mind', to the parade on 4 August.

Tomás and many others were adamant that the Volunteers should have one purpose only – to serve Ireland. He was asked by the executive committee in Dublin to make it quite clear that the Volunteers would not be helping England, but would be defending Ireland's shores against any armed forces that might come from any other nation. There were many statements issued from both sides but the matter was eventually brought to a close when the following article appeared in the *Cork Examiner:*

Sir,

In view of the statements of alleged dissensions in the Irish volunteers of Cork City the following resolution was passed on 5 August. It was unanimously re-affirmed at yesterday's meeting of the executive Committee that the committee of the Cork City Corps of Volunteers approves of the proposal set forward by the Provisional Committee Irish National Volunteers and are prepared to act unanimously in accordance with their recommendation namely that the Irish National Volunteers are prepared to join with the Ulster Volunteers for the defence of Ireland.

T. Mac Curtáin

Hon. Sec.

The inevitable happened: the movement split into two groups – The Irish Volunteers and the National Volunteers. Tomás was very upset because nobody seemed to have learned anything from the past – how many times in the course of Irish history was the phrase 'divide and conquer' true? It was back to the drawing-board again.

Elizabeth could see that he was exhausted – the effort he had put into the organisation on the committee side, let alone when it came to the work that went into the expansion of the Volunteers, was overwhelming. His efforts over the next twelve months would have to be doubled.

Many men who worked hard from dawn to dusk then turned around and spent hours training on a voluntary basis. Everything from basic training upwards was provided. Chains of command were put in place. Structures and procedures re-evaluated. Accounts systems were implemented for the purchase of arms and uniforms from donations and subscriptions. They would not, and could never, consider asking these men to take up arms for the empire and go to France or elsewhere to fight for the rights of small nations, while Ireland had no rights as a nation. Ireland needed the Volunteers. Surely, when it came to the freedom of a small nation, Ireland was their first priority. Her men were needed for her own freedom.

English government agents were watching the situation developing within the Volunteer organisation closely. Many Volunteers knew if they did not flee to America they would be imprisoned or sent into indefinite exile. The British banished a number of influential Volunteer leaders overseas but a core remained, in fact it consisted of approximately sixty volunteers and with their help Tomás worked tirelessly to rebuild the Irish Volunteer Force, Óglaigh na hÉireann.

The leaders had learned the necessity for cohesive organisation in the past, so the new force began with a very strong set of skills and with an effective system in place.

Meanwhile the National Volunteers were riding on the back of the support they had received with the public controversy between the two groups. It stimulated debate in many homes and public places around the country and gave the public a choice as to which organisation to join.

> The leaders had learned the need for cohesive organisation in the past, so the new force began with a very strong set of skills and an effective system in place.

ONE OF THE STATEMENTS ISSUED BY TOMÁS ON BEHALF OF THE VOLUNTEERS

The November anniversary of the Manchester Martyrs marked a turning point. Tomás and his fellow leaders reaped the benefit of the hard work – all the training and manoeuvres paid off. The Volunteers marched holding their heads high. Major John MacBride complimented them and aligned himself with their stance, and this public acknowledgement was very encouraging. Tomás and Terry MacSwiney, for a short time, basked in the glow of accomplishment and in the pride of their men.

6

The Split

The split between the two volunteer groups was further complicated by a controversy over funds. John Horgan representing the National Volunteers and Liam de Róiste, representing the Irish Volunteer Force were disputing the ownership of the collected finances and the press gave much publicity to the squabbles of the two groups. Both sides were claiming money which had been collected for the defence of Ireland fund. Accusations of wrong-doings started to fly. Tomás listened to the views of all and as financial squabbles continued between the two groups of Volunteers, he tried to maintain cordial pathways of communication as he busied himself with the training of the men. The publication of the audited balance sheet with its explanatory notes were distributed and that was the end of the matter as far as he was concerned.

Nights were spent in the kitchen with Terry Mac and many

others debating and thrashing out the actions of Volunteer movement in the past, present and future, and the bigger picture of Ireland as a nation. The dreamers, talkers, planners, thinkers, military strategists all had a part to play and a voice to be heard. Many a night Elizabeth went to bed with her head reeling with plans for their dream – which she and Tomás believed was close to becoming a reality – of a free Ireland.

> The dreamers, talkers, planners, thinkers, military strategists all had a part to play and a voice to be heard.

Within the National Volunteer movement and the Irish Volunteer movement, the leaders of each were aware that both organisations were going to welcome Douglas Hyde, the president of the Gaelic League, to Cork on 15 December. Tomás thought it was great that both groups, which had been so fractious throughout the year stood, if not side by side, at least in the one parade. John Horgan on one side with the National Volunteers and Seán O'Sullivan on the other with the Irish Volunteers.

If Ireland as a nation did not learn from her past, the same could be said for the British government. Having received the support of the National Volunteers for the war effort, it showed total disregard for its leaders and its ethos. They were a regiment of men who wished to keep their identity, have their leaders acknowledged and serve the cause of the crown together. But the National Volunteers continued to be taken for granted and treated with indifference by many in the British establishment.

As 1915 began, Tomás and his comrades took their minds off the world situation for a time and focused on Cork. The reorganisa-

tion after the split had taken its toll. Everyone involved was exhausted but things seemed to be running smoothly now. The men knew
their roles. Discipline and training came easy to them. The various
systems of reporting and accounting worked. Of course, all sympathisers would not make soldiers; so diverse roles were given to people
who wanted to help. The pipe band was a way for many to march
and show support. A group of Volunteers in the band ordered silver
Tara brooches from Dublin to wear on their pipe band uniforms
as they felt the brooch was a symbol of their heritage. Tomás had a
beautiful set of pipes made with ivory tops and his name engraved
on the circle. Elizabeth played the family concertina to him and the
children at home and when Tomás had any free time, he loved to
accompany her on his violin.

Frank Daly, a friend in the Volunteers, feared for Tomás' financial security as he was now a person of note in the city and Frank

knew that Suttons were unhappy employing a person who was so much in the limelight. Tomás could be seen on a regular basis on parade and he was vocal in his views that the British had no place in Ireland. Frank believed that the directors were about to ask for his resignation, at best, or possibly fire him. Premises came up for sale in Blackpool – a large unit comprising a shop opening onto the street at 40 Thomas Davis Street; a mill and flax factory to the back with plenty of room for expansion and more accommodation than the family would ever need. Tomás and his brother Seán discussed the advantages of purchasing the building. They were confident it would prove to be a profitable business. Elizabeth was reluctant to leave the area of the city where they were living and where they had spent so many happy times. She loved her home but agreed that a move was the right decision for the family and believed that the security and happiness of her family came first.

Tomás, Elizabeth and the children moved to 40 Thomas Davis Street to start what they hoped would be a new life in the business world. Things were not easy and money was scarce but the mill helped to keep expenses down. Seán, Tomás' brother, had a large shop in Shandon Street and would be involved as a partner in this new venture. Some of the workers from the flax factory, whose husbands were in the British army, used to swarm around the children and Elizabeth's door at night, shouting abuse. Elizabeth could understand why they were annoyed but believed that they were misguided. The women in the factory were also suffering; jobs were hard to come by – plenty of cheap labour was available but Tomás and Seán believed that a fair day's work deserved a fair day's pay and gave the flax workers and the Artan clothes factory girls what were considered very good working conditions at that time.

Elizabeth could not believe the amount of information Tomás could keep stored in his head

Elizabeth could not believe the amount of information Tomás could keep stored in his head. He and his brother Seán were now running a business. Yet even when he was in the shop, he was, at any spare moment away from the counter, writing notes, jotting down ideas, sending and receiving messages. The place was like a railway station with the coming and goings. Volunteer officers from outlying areas would come in to consult with Tomás. A bed would be rustled up at short notice for one of lads. It was common to find them still up in the early hours of the morning thrashing out plans. Elizabeth had long ago learned it was wise to have a spare bed ready and an extra meal in the pot.

EVEN WHEN HE WAS IN THE SHOP, TOMÁS WAS, AT ANY SPARE MOMENT AWAY FROM THE
COUNTER, WRITING NOTES ...

Tomás knew that he could not accomplish his plans, or fulfil his dreams, without Elizabeth at his side. She understood him, even when he was silent. They worked as one unit – two halves that fully complemented each other. Many a time there was no need for words, they understood each other in sorrow and in happiness. They had certainly encountered the extreme of both emotions since they married and would do so again in the future.

Terence

7

Danger of Exile

In the autumn of 1914, and in the wake of the Redmond split, the Irish Volunteers held a national convention at which the movement was officially reorganised. As part of this restructuring military formations known as brigades were introduced and Tomás was elected as the commandant of the Cork brigade and Terry MacSwiney as the vice-commandant. Almost every hour of his days were now spent between Thomas Davis Street and the Volunteers Hall on Sheares Street. Elizabeth spent the time running the house, helping with the mill shop and the Artan clothing factory. The manufacturing of clothes was an expansion that he and Seán thought prudent.

Lizzie had loved where she lived before, the Mardyke area. It had been very peaceful, with its beautiful walks and parks for the children to play in and she found the industrial part of the city daunting, particularly as she had no friends in the area. In fact, the busy young mother did not seem to have any time for herself. The children, the mill and the time spent helping Tomás left her fit only for bed at the end of a long day.

The British government increased its targeting of nationalists. It had observers reporting on the growth of the movement who went about systematically, area-by-area, making life difficult for supporters. Many men were arrested and Tomás became concerned, knowing deep down that the situation was becoming very bleak. J. J. Walsh had been banished to England and prevented from returning to Cork under Defence of the Realm Act.

A plan of action was needed. One by one, the British government was picking off the leaders. Diarmuid Fawsitt was to be its next target. He faced jail or exile, so opted to go to America. Tomás was very conscious that the leaders were under pressure but the leaders, members or supporters did not stand alone. They felt that when under threat, you stayed in your county and the Volunteers stood alongside you for support. A fund was set up to support the families of exiles and prisoners.

Tomás seemed to turn any group of men into an organised cohesive unit. They gave him their respect and loyalty and his orders were never questioned. He insisted on commitment and got it and was astute enough to know and understand his men and recognise their talents and their limits.

The outward success of the Volunteers, and the parades on Patrick's Day and during May, put the spotlight further on the Volunteers and its leaders who already had a high profile. This affected Elizabeth and the children, more than Tomás ever realised. Many people, especially the women and mothers of the men who were serving in the British army, misunderstood Tomás' views on men joining the British army and going overseas. Tomás and his men, on occasions, got verbal abuse when they were on parade and pelted with whatever was at hand.

The display by Tomás and his brigade at the funeral of O'Donovan Rossa on 1 August 1915 was impressive. Never before had so many Volunteers walked in uniform and stood in silence to show respect. Glasnevin cemetery was over-run with Volunteers and Pádraig Pearse delivered his oration to a captive audience.

> Bursting with idealism and enthusiasm, a combination that was hard to resist, they had everything you could wish for in a man – soldier, poet, musician, writer – and they believed nothing could douse the burning fire of the passion for a free Ireland.

Every month a different event propelled the Volunteer movement forward. Terry became the full-time Volunteer organiser for Cork City and county area and Tomás accompanied him almost every week on a tour of outlying district units. Bursting with idealism and enthusiasm, a combination that was hard to resist, they had everything you could wish for in a man – soldier, poet, musician, writer – and they believed nothing could douse the burning fire of the passion for a free Ireland. Pádraig Pearse travelled around the country giving

moving orations. When in the south, he was accompanied by a well-trained and equipped party of Volunteers and, on occasion, the pipe band played. The eerie sound of the pipes and the passionate speeches kindled a fire in hearts that did not realise how much nationalist blood ran in their veins.

The success of Terry's recruitment was proving to be a double-edged sword – there were many more recruits but they had to be whipped into shape in the fastest possible time. Training and the need to follow procedures had to be instilled into the new battalions. The concept of following orders and reporting for duty did not come easy to some of the recruits. Tomás and Terry were strict

TOMÁS LEADING THE VOLUNTEERS TO THE FUNERAL OF O'DONOVAN ROSSA

enforcers of discipline and respect and believed that following an order instantly could save lives in a conflict situation.

Terry was acutely aware that both of them were marked men and they knew that surveillance by British intelligence had identified them as notable leaders wielding great influence over their men. They felt a move would be made to surprise them – but under what guise?

1915 was a 'watch and wait' period, with the Volunteers gaining strength day by day. Each recruit became more competent in his or her role.

Elizabeth worried for Tomás on a daily basis. Their house

was constantly searched at times that would cause the most disruption, between midnight and dawn was the norm. The police would arrive and at gun point everybody's bed would be searched. More often than not their mattresses were tossed to the floor and slashed. The tip of the guns glistened in the light of the candles and terrified the children. It was obvious that the purpose behind these searches was to cause as much disruption to the Mac Curtáin household as possible. It used to take hours to settle everybody back to bed and, eventually, to sleep. The mornings following these raids were extremely difficult as some sort of routine had to be kept for the children and Tomás and Elizabeth had a full day's work to face.

Their house was constantly searched … the tip of the guns glistened in the light of the candles and terrified the children.

The raids were especially difficult since the birth of their new son, Tomás, on 14 June. Patrick could never be replaced as their first-born son but the arrival of a baby boy was greeted with great joy.

Elizabeth's sister Mary had died and she and Tomás had taken her two children under their wing. One of the good things about the house in Blackpool was that it gave them the opportunity to offer these children a home. On the first floor there was enough room for the Mac Curtáins, and on the top floor there was plenty of room for Mary's children. Elizabeth's brothers and sisters stayed over on a regular basis. Her nephew Patrick was an exceptionally intelligent child. Tomás had many discussions with the brothers at the North Monastery where

Patrick went to school. They sang his praises: a dream student, eager to learn and possessing an almost photographic memory – with virtually no effort he excelled in every subject. His head was always stuck in a book, but not necessarily schoolbooks. His Aunt Susie once jokingly remarked that she had no idea where he might find a wife in later years as his hands and legs looked totally out of proportion with his body. Patrick assured her there was no need to worry as 'love is blind'!

There were always children around. School friends of Patrick called in and Siobhán's best friend Mairín Casey was like another daughter to Tomás and Elizabeth. From time to time Siobhán lost herself in her imagination and the stories she invented. These bouts of fantasy normally came after a period spent out at Ballyknockane with the Curtins. After threshing time, her stories were even more far-fetched. It was after one of these visits that Siobhán assured Mairín that there was every chance that the anti-Christ was going to visit during the night and whisk her away. The poor child couldn't sleep with terror. A rather irate Mr Casey called to the house, earnestly requesting that Elizabeth keep a rein on Siobhán and her tales and fantasies!

Tomás brought home one of the first copies of the Manifesto which was issued by the executive committee of the Irish Volunteers on 15 July 1915. Elizabeth made a cup of tea for them and called Annie and her brother Jimmy to listen to him read it. The document made clear the difficulties that the organisation and the men were facing:

> The British government has ordered four Irishmen to leave Ireland.
> No charge has been brought against them, no fault has been imputed
> to them, they have not been summoned to defend themselves before

any tribunal, and no explanation has been given. They have received peremptory written orders to leave Ireland, their own country, within seven days. They had received these orders from a British authority established by force in Ireland and not from any Irish authority.

The men, who have received this arbitrary sentence of banishment from Ireland, without trial of any kind, without any cause stated, complaint made, or warning given, are organising instructors and prominent officers of the Irish Volunteers. Three of them are Ulstermen, one of whom is a well known businessman in Belfast ...

It was a worrying development and the 'movement' had felt compelled to print the details. The people of Ireland needed to be made aware of what was going on. They knew they could be in this situation at any time. He continued:

The order of banishment, like deportation orders, is nominally given, under the Defence of the Realm Act by General Friend, on behalf of the military authorities. General Friend is, in these acts of hostility to the Irish Volunteers, required to act as the political agent of the Government ... For a long time before the banishment orders were issued on the twelfth of July, Mr Birrell's offic-

THE PRESENT CRISIS.

MANIFESTO

Issued by the Executive Committee of the Irish Volunteers, 15th July, 1915.

The British Government has ordered four Irishmen to leave Ireland. No charge has been brought against them, no fault has been imputed to them, they have not been summoned to defend themselves before any tribunal, no explanation has been given. They have received peremptory written orders to leave Ireland, their own country, within seven days. They have received these orders from a British authority established by force in Ireland, and not from any Irish authority.

The men who have received this arbitrary sentence of banishment from Ireland, without trial of any kind, without any cause stated, complaint made, or warning given, are **organising instructors and prominent officers of the Irish Volunteers.** Three of them are Ulstermen, one of whom is a well-known business man in Belfast.

The order for banishment, like previous deportation orders, is nominally given, under the Defence of the Realm Act by General Friend, on behalf of the military authorities. General Friend is, in these acts of hostility to the Irish Volunteers, required to act as the **political agent** of the Government. The orders of deportation and banishment directed to members of the Irish Volunteer organisation are, in fact, the continuation, under Mr. Birrell's direction, of the "Curragh revolt" under General Gough, the Clontarf centenary expedition under Mr. Harrel, now reinstated in the Government service, and the shooting down of unarmed citizens at Bachelor's Walk.

General Friend, in giving these orders, **acts entirely** at the instance of Mr. Birrell's subordinate officers. For a long time before the banishment orders were issued on the twelfth of July, Mr. Birrell's officers were instructed to keep a constant watch both by day and night on the organisers now sentenced to banishment, and to note and report all their words and movements. It was known to the members of the Irish Volunteer Council, before any action was taken by the military authorities, that the political authorities of Dublin Castle had decided to proceed against the men now ordered into exile.

The fact that Mr. Birrell's department had kept up the strictest surveillance over these men for several months past, shows that Mr. Birrell desired to obtain some evidence that might enable him to act against them by process of law, civil or martial. He failed to obtain any such evidence, and, having failed, he resorted to the purely arbitrary powers exercised nominally by the military authority. It is evident that, by this policy, Mr. Birrell's Government hopes either to intimidate the Irish Volunteers or to provoke them into acts of unconsidered resistance. The Government will not succeed in either respect. The Irish Volunteers will continue training and strengthening their organisation to the maximum of efficiency, and making themselves more and more worthy of the confidence and support of the Irish Nation.

ers were instructed to keep a constant watch both day and night on the organisers now sentenced to banishment and to note and report all their words and movements. It was known to the members of the Irish Volunteers Council, before any action was taken by the military authorities, that the political authorities at Dublin Castle had decided to proceed against the men now ordered into exile …

The fact that Mr Birrell's department had kept up the strictest surveillance over these men for several months past, shows that Mr Birrell desired to obtain some evidence that might enable him to act against them …

Tomás paused to let them digest what he had read. 'It is evident that by this policy, Mr Birrell's government hopes either to intimidate the Irish Volunteers or to provoke them into acts of unconsidered resistance. The Government will not succeed in either respect.' He took a deep breath and read the following extract with passion and from the heart:

The Irish Volunteers will continue training and strengthening their organisation to the maximum of efficiency, and making themselves more and more worthy of the confidence and support of the Irish Nation.

For a moment, Elizabeth thought he was going to stand up to read it, he delivered it with such emotion. Elizabeth and Jimmy could see the obvious satisfaction that the statement gave him. He would be part of the building of that force. He would guide it and watch it growing from strength to strength … 'the war crisis had not alleviated the condition of affairs in Ireland that made the Irish Volunteer organisation necessary for the safety of Ireland. It had not altered the policies and purpose of the Irish Volunteer organisation. Now, more than in 1913, it is obvious that Ireland requires self-protection against the menace of armed force from whatsoever quarter. The future prosperity, perhaps the very existence of the Irish Nation, may depend on the country being in a position to offer effective resistance to the imposition of a ruinous burden of taxation from Imperial purposes.'

He would be part of the building of that force. He would guide it and watch it growing from strength to strength.

Tomás paused, again, but there was nothing for anybody around the table to add. He finished reading the last paragraph and they all then sat in total silence. Each was very much aware that it might have been the men in the north who had spurred the issuing of this document but Tomás, Jimmy, Seán or any of the lads in Cork could be exiled at any moment.

8

Easter 1916

They rang in the New Year with Terry Mac and as Tomás said, 'They could be well pleased with the growth of the movement'. The Manchester Martyrs' parade towards the end of the past year had given a very public display of how far they had come and the compliments from Seán Mac Dermott, given publicly during his oration and also given privately, still rang in their ears. They could not afford to bask in the glory of their achievements as each was very aware that they were still ill-equipped, and had a long way to go in training the Volunteers. Tomás tried to bring everybody back to reality and explained that success was going to be achieved slowly – one step at a time.

There had been some discussions with James Connolly, the leader of the Citizen Army, as to what the English might do and everyone needed to be made aware of the risks. Elizabeth's brother Tommy was a follower of Connolly and kept the household up to date with all the information he could gather. Tomás knew that Tommy intended to go to Dublin and 'lend a hand' whenever the call came but at this time all were unaware of what Pearse and the others had planned.

Tomás rushed home to Elizabeth one afternoon with the news that Terry MacSwiney and Thomas Kent had been arrested. He had warned Terry that he thought some move would be made after the inflammatory speeches they had given at Ballynoe. Terry Mac was held on remand for just over a month, and when released he and Tomás made arrangements for the St Patrick's Day parade. Tension was high and they knew they were being watched constantly. Just before St Patrick's Day Tomás and Elizabeth's home was raided, yet again, in the middle of the night and Tomás was very concerned about Elizabeth because she was pregnant. He had nothing incriminating in the house but once more, the raid disrupted the household.

> They could not afford to bask in the glory of their achievements as each was very aware that they were still ill-equipped, and had a long way to go in training the Volunteers.

The couple were shocked by the record of events published in the *Cork Constitution* implying that members of the National Volunteers had given information to the authorities that led to the most recent spate of raids. Could this really be true? Both groups had their different perspectives on events that led to the split, but did the National Volunteers actually report the activities of the Irish Volunteers to the British authorities knowing that this would lead to house raids and arrests? Elizabeth found it hard to believe.

Tomás felt the reports were being created to inflame the tension that existed among the different groups leading up to the St Patrick's celebrations. He was adamant that if trouble broke out his men would not have any part in it. He would do everything possible to ensure that the parade passed peacefully.

With this in mind, he issued the following order:

Irish Volunteers – Cork Brigade

St. Patrick's Day Demonstration in Cork City, 1916

Your Company is to parade at full strength, and with full equipment, and one day's rations, at above parade in Cork City.

The Brigade will be inspected by an officer of the Headquarters Staff, and special attention will be paid to the conditions of arms.

For train arrangements, enquire of the local stationmaster.

Companies will be met on arrival by officers of the Brigade Staff.

Officers will please note the following Orders, which must be strictly adhered to: –

(1) Any breach of discipline must be severely dealt with and not let pass unnoticed.

(2) On no account will any man leave ranks without permission from his officer.

(3) Any man using ammunition without an order, either before, during, or subsequent to this parade, is to be immediately deprived of his arms, suspended from the organisation, and case reported to the Brigade Council for investigation.

Note – The special attention of all ranks is called to above order.

(4) On arrival at Cork all officers will take orders from officers of the Brigade Staff, who will wear a Blue Band round cap.

(5) Any man under the influence of drink will be considered incapable, deprived of his arms and equipment, and forthwith suspended from the organisation, pending trial by courtmartial.

(6) Every volunteer is responsible for the honour of the Brigade, and should bear himself accordingly.

By Order of Brigade Council,

T. Mac Curtáin,

Commandant

Elizabeth insisted on going with all the children and her extended family. She wanted to show her support for the Irish Volunteers, and she wanted to be there for Tomás. She was sure that with wives and children present it would be less likely that any trouble would start. She was right, the St Patrick's Day parade passed without any remarkable incident and the Volunteers marched with great pride. The household at Blackpool ended the outing with a special tea. Elizabeth settled thoroughly exhausted, happy children down to bed that night. They were delighted at 'seeing Daddy as a soldier'.

Easter 1916

Tomás was aware that there was some plot emerging from Dublin but felt very frustrated as he had received no details. On Palm Sunday, orders arrived from Dublin outlining his and Terry's role. He understood from his orders that there would be a landing of

THE VOLUNTEERS HALL ON SHEARES STREET

arms in Kerry and that he was to provide an armed escort. He was under strict instruction that information was to be passed on only on a need to know basis. On 9 April, he told the relevant officers about their roles. The men thought they were going on an exercise, but the distribution of first aid kits and instructions to ready themselves from Tomás left them in no doubt that things had reached a different level. Although not sure of what was going to happen, they were aware that some real action was about to take place.

What was not known at this time was that Joseph Plunkett and Seán Mac Dermott had forged 'the Castle document' which gave details of how the British authorities intended to suppress the Irish Volunteer movement. If any Volunteer still did not burn with passion, this document certainly instilled the desire to fight. It was clear that there would be a fight ahead – whatever circumstances would trigger it. The Volunteers thought that they were to be suppressed forcefully and almost to a man decided to stand their ground.

Tomás received the order to have his men ready on Holy Thursday but then began receiving conflicting reports. Eoin MacNeill, chief of staff, was furious that he did not know the full plan for the Rising and he sent an order to cancel the original order. Pádraig Pearse issued instructions that 'now was the time' and MacNeill's orders were to act only where there was no other option – when confronted by action from the crown forces.

Pearse and Mac Dermott had to get MacNeill's agreement that the Rising was going to happen – and it was now or never. J.J. O'Connell, with instructions from Eoin MacNeill, was on his way to Cork and the *Aud* was on its way to Ireland with arms. MacNeill felt that he now had no option but fall in with the insurrection but he was still furious with Pearse as he felt he, and others on the executive committee of the Volunteers, should have been involved in this plan. MacNeill tried quickly to get Volunteer Jim Ryan to Cork to tell Tomás that the original plan was now back in action.

Tomás was in turmoil as he was receiving conflicting orders and instructions. He went to Mallow to meet O'Connell from the train and discovered that O'Connell had gone to Cork. By the time Tomás returned to Cork he found him at Terry Mac's house on Victoria Road. On foot of MacNeill's order O'Connell took over command of the Volunteers and the action was cancelled, not only in Cork but also in the rest of Munster.

Casement arrived in Kerry and was arrested. The leaders in Kerry, Austin Stack and Con Collins, were also arrested and sent to prison on Spike Island. This rendered Kerry useless to the Rising and the Kerry Volunteer units were now without direction. When the ship was captured and was being led to Cobh, the captain scuttled her and the much-needed arms sank to the bottom of the sea close to Cork harbour. The Rising was on, then off, then when Jim Ryan arrived, it was all back on again. Tomás sent word back to Dublin that he would do what he could, but he was aware that any plans or orders were now completely compromised. He had units marching all over the county, in full view of the British forces.

Tomás was always so organised – everything was planned and all possible circumstances that might arise were thought out in advance so that his men always knew there would be a back-up plan. This was alien territory for such a methodical man. Everything was so disorganised, disjointed, with orders countermanding orders. He depended on getting accurate information and instructions but this was not happening. He was back in command of the men but unsure of how exactly he was to instruct them.

News reached MacNeill on Easter Saturday that Casement had been arrested and the *Aud* had sunk and he felt that there was no chance of any success with military action at this time. Even with the German arms which the *Aud* had been carrying, the Volunteers were still going to be ill-equipped and the whole Volunteer movement had very little with which to defend themselves.

Tomás could not believe what he heard from MacNeill. All action was now to be cancelled again, but it was too late as he had already given the order for military action and there would be utter confusion if he ordered his men to a stand down now.

Tomás and Terry assessed the situation. They had no idea what was going on in Dublin. Rumours were rampant. The men were marching all over the county and he wondered were they marching, on his command, to their certain deaths? There was no cohesive plan and arms were in short supply. Having had discussions with Terry and other men, Tomás felt he had absolutely no option at this stage but to issue a stand down order. It was nearly impossible to get orders around the county quickly. The weather conditions were horrendous but men were sent, by whatever transport was available, to tell the Volunteers that all prior orders were cancelled. They were to stand down, go home and wait for further instructions.

> The men were marching all over the county and he wondered were they marching, on his command, to their certain deaths?

Elizabeth waited at home for Tomás. He had left the house on Saturday morning saying 'I will see you later darling'. He normally told her if he expected to be away overnight. There was an air of readiness in the city and the tension was almost palpable. Volunteers in uniform had been moving around the city. Elizabeth thought that they moved with more purpose than usual. There seemed to be a spring in their step. Tomás, getting dressed and leaving the house that morning, had been in a very sombre mood and she thought he lingered longer than normal kissing them all goodbye. Was her imagination playing tricks on her?

At various stages, Volunteers arrived from outlying districts looking for him. No. 40 Thomas Davis Street was like the nerve centre of the movement. Their first stop was normally the mill and, depending on the urgency of their journey, they would grab a hot meal and head off to where Elizabeth directed them, usually to the hall in Sheares Street. As she was going to bed, she saw from her upstairs window a number of Volunteers going home. She thought manoeuvres were over and was expecting Tomás but, as she waited throughout the night, he did not return.

Her brother Tommy had gone to Dublin to serve in the Citizens Army. She later learned that he had joined up with Connolly's men and was based at the corner of Sackville [O'Connell] Street and Abbey Street. He was dressed in his new uniform and was on duty on Easter Monday. A group of his friends from Cork passed up the road and started kicking his newly erected barricade. When Tommy went over to stop them they recognised him and started shouting, 'well look who we have here – good old Corkie Walsh' addressing him by his nickname. They continued ribbing him, kicking the barricade and causing general disorder. Corkie fired his gun into the air to disperse them. History would

Tommy

LEFT: TOM O'SULLIVAN AND DIARMUID O'SHEA AND RIGHT: TOMÁS AND TERENCE ON MANOEUVRES WITH THE VOLUNTEERS

record that Corkie Walsh fired the first shot of the Easter Rising near the GPO. The circumstances did not get a mention!

Tomás had asked a young Volunteer to get word to Elizabeth that he had gone to Ballingeary to talk with Seán O'Hegarty, the leader of the IRB in the southern area. He was distraught with worry for his men and knew the British authorities would be well aware of the confusion. Tomás worked on the principle that since he had informers and methods of finding out what the authorities were up to, they in turn would have their informers. He never ceased to be amazed at how easy it was to procure information. Having a postmistress steam open letters sent to officials might seem a very basic way of acquiring information, but it worked. Off-duty officials could often be encouraged to loosen their tongues by a few drinks.

On Monday night he and his fellow officers had no idea that the Rising had taken place in Dublin and it was only on his return

Cork IRA officers: Front from Left: Tadhg Barry, Tomás Mac Curtáin, Pat Higgins
Back row: David Cotter, Seán Murphy, Donal Barrett, Terence MacSwiney, Paddy Trahey

to Cork that he heard what had happened. On going to the hall, he received the orders that Pearse had sent, saying they would rise at noon on Easter Monday. Even that order was peculiar in that it was written on a scrap of paper, not signed just initialled.

The rumour machine gathered momentum. Tomás was hearing many stories – all related about third-hand: a hundred became a thousand soldiers, shots became battles and he was utterly perplexed as to the reality of the situation. In the cold light of day, there were no arms and no men as he had sent them all home. There were no definite orders and there was most certainly no plan – there was no right decision. He felt utterly responsible for the future of his men and alone in the knowledge that his next command could send hundreds to their death.

He did believe that by now they had shown their hand and that any action would be severely dealt with by the forces of the crown. There was to be no attack or rising in Cork but they would stay at the hall to defend it – headquarters would not be vacated and the men would occupy the building. Michael Leahy, who was in charge of the Volunteers from Cobh and Maurice Aherne, an officer from Dungourney, travelled to Cork and went to the hall at Sheares Street. Tomás issued orders that nobody from the crown forces was to be allowed to enter the hall and that force should be used if this was attempted. Should it prove necessary to defend and retain Sheares Street by force, it would be the first military act of defiance in Cork.

Elizabeth got the news and was sick with worry as Tomás was surrounded in the hall and she could not decipher fact from fiction in the stories reaching them at the mill.

Word was spreading regarding the action in Dublin. T. C. Butterfield, the Lord Mayor and James Crosbie in Cork contacted Brigadier General Stafford to try to stall any British action in Cork. They hoped that Tomás and his men could be 'talked' out of the hall and thus ensure that there would be no loss of life. Capt. Wallace Dickie was appointed the negotiator and a meeting was arranged with Bishop Cohalan. They sent word that they would like to talk to Mac Curtáin. They ascertained that Tomás did not intend to start a military action but if there was to be a move against him or his men, they would be forced to take up arms and defend themselves.

Word came to Tomás in the hall that a number of British units were deployed and ready to fire if necessary. The bishop and the negotiator thrashed out an agreement to put to Tomás. The understanding of the agreement was that if the arms were given to the Lord Mayor or the bishop no action would be undertaken by the British. The message Tomás received was different: if the Volunteers did not surrender, they would be shelled. The bishop intervened and pointed out that this was not the case.

Negotiations went back and forth and it was eventually agreed that the Volunteers would hand up their arms but that these arms would remain their property. There would be no publicity and a general amnesty would be granted. Tomás and Terry had little choice but to agree to do this and left to make sure that other areas knew what was happening. They travelled around the county, and other parts of Munster, to let the Volunteers know what was going on in Cork. They arrived back in Cork to discover that details had been printed in the *Constitution* newspaper even though part of the agreement said there would be no publicity. Tomás took this to be a blatant breach of the agreement and felt he could not ask the Volunteers to hand over their arms without safeguards. The bishop was very upset and the negotiator assured him that though the British government could not be seen to be making an agreement, the essence of the agreement would be implemented. He convinced the bishop to accompany him back to Sheares Street hall to talk to the Volunteers. The delegation, including the Lord Mayor T. C. Butterfield, addressed the men and they agreed to hand over their arms to the Lord Mayor.

Men left the hall, some to hand over the arms personally to the Lord Mayor's home and some to go home. Tomás, Terry and the other leaders were bitterly disappointed at the developments of the week and felt they had totally let down the men in Dublin. The only ray of light was that there had been no bloodshed in Cork and the men were able to go home with an understanding that their arms would be returned when this crisis was over and there would be no reprisal action against any Volunteer. Armed struggle would have been futile as there was absolutely no possibility of a victory.

9

Broken Word

On his return home, Tomás reassured Elizabeth and asked her not to worry. He told her about the 'comings and goings' at Sheares Street and the various meetings with the negotiators. She was worried that he might be arrested and even shot. He reassured her repeatedly that there was an agreement in place which the bishop and the Lord Mayor had witnessed and not even the British authorities would dare break their word in this case. But Elizabeth was right to be worried. General Sir John Maxwell ordered a total crackdown at the end of April and the homes of Volunteers were raided systematically. Tomás, his brother Seán and a number of other Volunteers were arrested.

The bishop was appalled. He could not believe that the authorities would go back on their word. So little time had elapsed since he had stood side by side with the authorities and promised the Volunteers that there would be no arrests. He set out to negotiate the release of the men. Many were released, including Tomás, but agreements had been broken and promises forgotten. There was no honour. History had once again been repeated – the English establishment did not keep its word.

Although Tomás was free again, for the present, arrests were taking place all around him. Pearse and his comrades in Dublin had been executed. He was devastated. Elizabeth busied herself around the house to try to keep her mind off the events in Dublin. 'There but for the will of God', she thought.

The British rounded up not just Volunteers but sympathisers and Tomás felt guilty that he had not been arrested and held with his men. Elizabeth felt as though she was walking on eggshells. There was no right thing to say to him. Normally they could talk events through and agree on the outcome but in this case, he kept mulling over the choices he had made, questioning indeed if there had been a choice or had he let down Pearse? Even though they talked about the actions of Easter week, Tomás relived the events of the week repeatedly, looking for an answer. Elizabeth felt there weren't any answers. Her brother Jimmy had tried to set his mind at rest by telling Tomás that as a leader he had done all that was possible and even enlisted Seán to reassure his brother, and try to lift him out of his gloom.

> Tomás and Terry knew that a ground-swell of support was increasing. The people in the street were now talking about a free Ireland and the Easter proclamation.

Tomás and Terry knew that a ground-swell of support was increasing. The people in the street were now talking about a free Ireland and the Easter proclamation. The executions of the leaders meant that the stance they had taken at the GPO would never be forgotten. When they were shot, there was an outpouring of astonishment and anger. Many now shared the dream of a free Ireland and the outcry from the ordinary citizens could only benefit the Volunteers. Work would have to be done to capitalise on this new-found support but it was difficult, considering the state the Volunteer force was in.

Word had come through to Elizabeth that her brother Tommy had been arrested in Dublin after the Rising. Jimmy had been arrested the week earlier. As far as Elizabeth could find out both had been sent to Richmond but she had no confirmation of this. She knew that as soon as it was possible one of them would write and it was enough for her now to know that they were alive. She thanked God neither of them had been shot.

The 11 May seemed no different to any other day. Tomás was overseeing the factory and had worked late the night before on organisational matters for the Volunteers. He was trying to keep track of his men: who had been arrested, had they been charged, sentenced, etc. It was vital that the families were kept informed as the arrests would hit some of the country farms very badly as sometimes all the men from one household could be gone. He was bone-weary and very despondent with all that was happening especially because young Volunteers continued to be arrested on a daily basis. He felt guilty because he had negotiated a pact that was meant to ensure their freedom and look where that had landed them!

No. 40 Thomas Davis Street was raided again that day and Tomás was arrested in front of the family. The children were very upset and there was no consoling Susie, Elizabeth's sister. She cried bitter tears and just could not contain herself. There was noise coming from everywhere, as the rooms were ransacked. Elizabeth remained amazingly calm as Tomás was being taken away, kissing him on the cheek, smiling and saying 'have courage'. These words were to stay with him and, as he told her afterwards, were a great source of comfort to him. He was brought to the barracks, searched and his belongings were taken, but he was allowed to keep one little book, *The Imitation of Christ*. The days in the detention barracks passed slowly. When the prisoners met in the prison yard they were not allowed speak to each other and nobody knew what the outcome of their incarceration might be.

'Have courage'... these words were to stay with him and, as he told her afterwards, were a great source of comfort to him.

Elizabeth heard that they were moving Tomás and the men. She sent word to as many relatives and Volunteers as she could through a network that had been developed, and members of Cumann na mBan helped spread the news. She had little time to prepare as she only heard the news late on 21 May that all the prisoners were to be moved very early the following morning.

Elizabeth, Susie, and many other relatives of the imprisoned men went to the jail gates. At about 8 a.m., Tomás and his men left the detention barracks to go to the railway station. They put on a brave front and a strained air of joviality barely masked the worry etched on all their faces. Elizabeth knew that this was a show for the families and worried even more about the fate of her husband. She did not get a chance to talk to him and would not give the guards the satisfaction of pushing her back if she tried.

Elizabeth was sick with worry for Tomás. She feared that sending the men to Dublin meant that they were to be executed. There was no doubting that Tomás held a pivotal position within the freedom movement and she thought that if they were going to execute more leaders Tomás and Terry would surely be next. Dreadful as it was to be parted, the news that they were being sent overseas was greeted with almost a sense of relief; at least they would be alive.

In a way, it seemed as if the British authorities believed that the theory 'out of sight was out of mind' would work. They felt that the rounding up and imprisonment of the men would return the situation in Ireland to what they considered to be normal.

Tomás recorded in his diary:

We were kept waiting for a long time in the barrack yard. One of the officers in charge of us went to speak to one of the local officers and we were brought into a large hall or gymnasium and given some sort of tack in a large bucket, bread and 'bully' beef. We lay down on the ground and ate it. We were then put into a big barrack room. I was in Barrack Room N1. There were twenty-four in the room and each was given three blankets and were told to sleep on the floor. I forgot to mention that we left the brother of Thomas Kent behind us in Cork, but I heard later that my wife Eilís brought in food and drink for him as long as he was there. This gave me great satisfaction. This was a new type of life alto-gether for us – there were great crowds of prisoners here. Peadar Ó hAnnracháin, Traolach Mac Suibhne, Austin Stack, Con Collins, Eoin MacNeill, Count Plunkett and thousands of others. There was a plentiful supply of food and drink given to us here. The soldiers in charge of us here were mainly Notts and Derbys, they were hardly able to speak and when they did it was mainly curses and filthy language they used. 'Ten on yer' they would say when accompanying us to the latrines and that was some place, there was no toilet paper there for us. Every second day prisoners were being sent to England. I had two masses there and these were held in the open air, with the soldiers all round with their guns and bayonets. The soldiers would look at us in amazement and at the priest as Mass was going on. I doubt if they had any religion at all ... We had Mass on Sunday and another day during the week. We thought at first that the men from Cork would not be sent to England since we were in a special place near the cook house, N.I., but things were not as we thought.

On Wednesday 31 May 1916 we got orders to prepare ourselves to cross the Irish Sea to England. Each of us received a haversack and after three hours of counting and preparation we headed to Kingsbridge Station and crossed the bridge there and down the left bank of the River Liffey. The people gathered and followed, and by the time we reached O'Connell Bridge, thousands gathered around us and they shouted, roared and cursed the soldiers – they were vicious against the soldiers. At last we reached the North Wall. On our way there we noticed the results of the 1916 rising, houses were in ruins around Sackville (O'Connell) St. and the Bridge. Bullet marks on all the houses and shops, huge holes in walls done by the heavy artillery – the place in ruins, destroyed as if hit by an earthquake.

We went on board ship at the North Wall and were put in amongst the cattle. I was afraid of getting seasick and I stayed in the air near the hold. Many more came out to where I was so that they could get their last glimpse of Ireland and everyone pretended not to be the least bit worried, but it was easy to see that behind all the banter and humour that they were really worried.

With Éire gone out of sight, quietness came over everyone, the good humour and merriment disappeared. Each was thinking when he would be back home or if ever he would. Further trouble awaited as those inside began to get sick, grew paler and paler and were forced to lie down somewhere. There was great silence now and those who were not sick were afraid of their lives of getting sick.

I didn't get sick as the place I was in, out in the air, agreed with me and so I stayed there. It got cold around 12.00 and the cold went through me, but I preferred the cold to the sickness so I stayed where I was. All but a few on the ship were sick. Tom Walsh was on the boat as well and we were both in Richmond together, but when we alighted in Holyhead, Tom was sent to Nuttsford and I was taken to Wakefield. His brother and my wife's brother Jimmy had been in Richmond for a few days but he was brought back to Cork and the Justice gave him two months in prison. Anyway when we alighted in Holyhead the cold really got to me. We were divided up and myself, Traolach, Peter O'Dwyer and about a hundred more were sent to Wakefield and the rest were sent to Nuttsfield. A train was waiting for us in Holyhead and we left at one o' clock. We reached Wakefield around ten o' clock. We were tired out and after being

> With Éire gone out of sight, quietness came over everyone, the good humour and merriment disappeared.

examined etc., we were brought to our cells at eleven. Some of us were in AI which was next to Áilbhe Ó Cadháin, Liam Ó Dúgáin, Seán Ó hAnnracháin, Maurice Aherne, Con Aherne, Ed Barrett, etc. it was the worst possible place in the prison. The flagstones in all the cells were wobbly and as old as the hills and were falling apart. Each time you put your foot on one of them a pall of dust would rise from the flags. It was BAD. The first day was bad enough and in the evening I got internal pains and as well as that I had diarrhoea. The coldness of the journey, across the Irish Sea, which went through my bones, must have been the cause. I sent for a doctor and asked him to have me removed to the top of the house – Aherne was his name – I heard he was from Cork. He took no interest in me and he gave me some stuff that only made me worse and instead of shifting me to the top of the house he just changed me to the other side of the hall, the same hall. This cell was as bad as the other one but had one advantage. In the first cell you were the last to be served your meals. The food was always cold and the soup would be cold and like dripping. In my new cell I was served first and it was an improvement, even though the food was always bad and if we were depending on these meals solely we would be in a bad state, but we were not depending on the gaol food. Many people came to visit us and they would bring food, tobacco and such things and these visitors would include nuns and priests who worked locally. I was unable to eat anything and the internal pains grew worse by the day. I asked one of the two priests who came in if he could bring in a naggin of brandy, having told him of the internal pains and being unable to eat. He said he would do his best. I sent many letters home that week to the people who used to visit us. A few days later the priest came in and gave me a bottle of brandy and when I went in after his visit I took a few drops and I felt improved immediately.

On Friday the 9th all the prisoners were called out. And from them a hundred men were called out, including myself, and almost all the men in AI. We were told to get ready to move … At first I thought we were being sent home, as one of the soldiers told me this, but I had my doubts. Eventually, we learned that we were being sent to Fronngach.

Papers were put before us to sign and we were told that a place was ready for us there in Fronngach in north Wales. I did not like Wakefield one bit, to be sure I was sick while I was there, but apart from that I hated the place. It was thronged with prisoners and we were able to go from place to place or should I say from yard to yard. In my opinion it was a miserable dark and unhealthy place. I was delighted leaving the place even though we did not know what was in store for us in Fronngach, all I had in Wakefield was mis-direction and misfortune.

We left Wakefield on Saturday morning, 10 June 1916 at 10.00 a.m. and went by train to Fronngach in north Wales. The guards of the Cameron highlanders were all around us and escorted us. These soldiers were pleasant enough and one in particular who accompanied Liam Duggan and myself – Liam was from Dunmanway. We went through Manchester, etc. to Balla and then about four miles to Fronngach. The people in the various stations would look at us in amazement. When we came to Chester one of the station workers enquired of the soldier in command of us and said, 'Irish rebels', isn't it?'

'Yes' said the guard.

'I hear,' said the station man, 'that they are going to rear up again on Monday next, i.e. Whit Monday. The man in charge did not answer. Eventually we reached Fronngach in the heart of the mountains and it was there that they took from me my note book that I had from the beginning and they would not return it.

Fronngach

We came into Fronngach on Saturday evening at about 6.00 p.m. It is a very small station and when we got off the train we saw the Camp next to the railway just next to us and completely surrounded with barbed wire. We saw the local onlookers walking up and down and each observing from his own patch. These were old soldiers and they were not capable of doing anything ... The Camp was an old distillery once and all the buildings were still there but now changed into one mighty spacious room, higgledy-piggledy style. The Germans were here before us and there were more than a thousand of them and there was not sufficient space for them there in the old buildings.

Since there was not sufficient room in the old buildings, timber huts were built outside each holding twenty men. There was a cook house, here, a place for washing clothes and big long rooms for sleeping. There was also a room for drying clothes and after being a week there it was full of ... and we did not put our clothes in there at all. There was a very big dining-room. There would be a thousand of us eating there. There was a similar Camp two hundred yards north of our one and that was full of prisoners as well. When both places were full they would hold one thousand eight hundred altogether. All around us were the mountains and some of them were covered with trees. The place was all right during summer, but when the rain came, and often it did, it was terrible.

Both Camps were situated well up the mountains. We were surrounded by mountains looking down on the Camps menacingly.

The soldiers were equipped with shotguns and this was very sensible in my opinion because when fired the pellets would scatter in all directions and could do lots of harm, but with a rifle they would have to take aim and this takes time. Many people in Ireland have no time for shotguns and they should have, because they are better and more suitable for certain people than the rifle. The officers' houses are just next to us but on the other side of the barbed wire …

Tomás' head was still in turmoil regarding the events of Easter week, the part he played and the affect his decisions had on hundreds of men.

German prisoners of war were moved out of the Old Distillery to make way for almost 2,000 Irish men. Having arrived and settled in, Tomás and Michael Collins discussed at length the rights and wrongs, shortcomings and general failure of the action of the past three years. They were allowed to mix and the leaders set about keeping the men busy. Classes were set up: Irish and history lessons given and an air of self-imposed discipline descended on the prison. Tomás and Michael put the time to good use and began to plan for the future.

Tomás' head was still in turmoil regarding the events of Easter week, the part he played and the affect his decisions had on hundreds of men. He relived the days, the discussions and the agreements. The 'what if's' played on his mind. He eventually came to the conclusion that if he had the same choices all over again he could do no different. He would not send men to fight a futile battle. At least they were alive and they would certainly take their chances the next time – and there would be a next time.

By the end of June, some of the Cork men were allowed home but not Tomás or Terry – there was no question of their release. He was surprised when two weeks later he was sent to Reading jail, and found Terry Mac in the adjoining cell.

News came through to the prisoners that Roger Casement had been found guilty of treason and was to be hung. Tomás put pen to paper to record his thoughts:

Rúairí Mac Easmann (Roger Casement)

Rúairí will be hanged tomorrow morning. He is a generous, faithful and loyal man, a real gentleman. What a pity, what a terrible pity.

May God grant you eternal peace Rúairí. I remember well speaking to him in Cork, in the Imperial Hotel – it was a great honour for me. I wouldn't doubt you England for carrying out this dirty deed, but the evil effects of this terrible deed will haunt you till Judgement Day – to the end of your reign and the sooner the better.

Thursday August 3rd 1916

'First keep thyself in peace and then shalt thou be able to bring peace to others'.
Roger Casement is going to his death now at 9 o'clock. May God give eternal peace to his soul. I wonder will they carry it out? Oh, it's a pitiful story and he such a noble and generous gentleman.

At the appointed time of the execution, Irish prisoners in English jails stood still. Word had spread that Casement would be hung

and it was agreed that all prisoners would stop whatever they were doing, be it work or pleasure and pray for the repose of his soul – one of their own was going to his Maker, may he rest in peace. A soldier was dying for the cause. Tomás knew where one fell another would most certainly take his place. That was the way it had always been and that was the way it would remain until Ireland was free.

Tomás wrote that night:

A newspaper arrived this evening and alas it read Casement was hanged this morning. Bad cess to the English for perpetrating such evil, they are the devil incarnate. I am of the opinion that as true as God is above they will pay for it later. His final words from the gallows were, 'I am going to death for my country'. There were three priests in attendance at his execution and he died a Catholic. We were shaking with anger when we read it. Poor Seán T. was cry-

Chorus of young Curtins "We want to be interned with Daddy"

DRAWING TAKEN FROM TOMÁS' AUTOGRAPH BOOK:
CHORUS OF YOUNG CURTINS 'WE WANT TO BE INTERNED WITH DADDY'

ing, Rúairí was such a fine noble man – may God have mercy on him, Jesus have mercy on him and may he be seated at the right hand of God.

Elizabeth and all at home wrote as often as they could and made little parcels for Tomás and the men. Cakes were made with tender loving care, then wrapped and sent. A good week was when they heard of somebody going on a visit. Food and gifts would be hastily put together to make a package. Socks and jumpers were knitted in anticipation of a cold winter.

Special photos were taken to send to her husband. She had written to tell him that they would be arriving soon and she knew the anticipation of receiving them was driving him crazy. Apparently, he had told the whole prison that he was expecting them. When they did arrive Tomás showed them around with great pride. He pointed out to everybody how well his Eilís looked and assured them that he knew what a lucky man he was to have married her.

Life in jail for him passed slowly and he kept himself busy reading and quoting Thomas à Kempis. Autograph books were

passed around. Many of the men spent hours wondering what to write, while others took the books and spent hours writing and sketching. Tomás got great pleasure reading the contributions in his book. He loved the sketch of the children crying for him and thought the drawing of Pearse was exceptional. He treasured his book and placed it with his other booklet, *The Imitation of Christ*, which had stayed with him all the time. He knew that Elizabeth would enjoy studying the autographs when he brought home the autograph book. Yes, he had to hold on to that thought – he would be going home.

On Wednesday 17 September 1916, he wrote to Elizabeth's brother, Tommy, who had been released earlier:

> ... I met Lizzie and 'tis then only life for me began, whether sorrow or joy, even heavy sorrow, loses its bitterness in perspective and when that sorrow is shared by a loyal and true partner a person looks back upon it as a victory over adversity and it becomes tinged with a feeling of having borne up well under trying difficulties and standing the test, of being tried and not found wanting. I only know now, after Lizzie who certainly is splendid when trouble knocks at the door. Thanks for your help and Siobhán's and Mary's (God rest her) and Sue's Ma's, in fact you all have been so good to me in some pretty serious difficulties which I have been up against for the past eight years; and greater than all the material assistance was the powerful use you always made of prayer on our behalf. I will always bless you for that. Forgive me again for rambling so much into my own affairs, but the mood happens to be on me and I like to say to you what really is in my mind ...

A reply arrived swiftly:

✝

Brigidine Convent,

Goresbridge,

Co. Kilkenny.

Sunday

5 Nov -16

Rec'd
9/16

my darling dadda
      thank you very
much for your lovely
letter. dont write any
more now till you
can easily. but write
to poor mama who
must be lonely.

PART OF SIOBHÁN'S LETTER TO TOMÁS

2 Moorfield Tce
4th Oct 1916,

… Received letter this evening and was delighted to get same. You
do not bother me with anything you say – rather I feel pleasure
to have you speak out your mind. Lizzie was here (you know she
comes to Moorfield every Sunday and Wednesday). So I succeed-
ed in getting her to write that promised letter. I dare say you will
have both together. 'Tis hard for her to manage writing for when
Tomás Óg sees her, he wants to go to her. He is trotting around
now, but has to be well watched. The darling is up to all sorts of
mischief. He went over to my book case today and made a great
haul. You should hear the attempt he made to tell me all about it
when I went to scold him …

Tomás was delighted with the news from home and read and re-
read both letters. He missed Elizabeth and the children intensely,
but this was his lot and he would just have to live with it. Elizabeth
most definitely had her hands full being at home with the children, and so much work to do.

Tomás wrote to Siobhán and it broke his heart to read her
reply dated Sunday 5 November 1916 which he received on the
ninth:

My darling dada,
Thank you very much for your lovely letter, don't write to me any
more now till you can easily but write to poor mama who must be
lonely. You will be glad to hear I made my first confession a short
time ago. the priest told me it was a very good one. Maybe i will
be let have first communion before christmas … my very best love
to you, darling dadda your own wee siobhán.

Elizabeth felt Christmas was going to be a very lonesome time.
There was talk of an amnesty but by mid December there was no
news of Tomás or Terry coming home. Tomás Óg was now a year

and a half old, and his older sisters, Siobhán and Síle, adored him. In a house with many of adults coming and going, they always found time to play with him. Jimmy and Tommy had been released and she prayed every night that Tomás would be home soon.

In the meantime, her husband was thinking what a difficult time this was for Elizabeth. Christmas would only just be over and the anniversary of their stillborn child would lie heavy on her mind. Tomás' heart went out to her as their baby son Patrick's anniversary would dampen any festivities:

> Now after eight years, I look back
> And know there is no woman in Ireland
> As loyal as you
> My love for you, Eilís, deepens in the face of
> Every difficulty, forever deepening until death ...

With him away, her loneliness was fierce. In his prison cell, he faced the prospect of a lonesome Christmas in exile. What could he say to her? He so wanted to be with her. Words failed him. He could write nothing to help her during this time, so he sent her a short note and also wrote to his baby son:

22.XII.16
To Tomás Óg Mac Curtáin

My dearest child
I am happy in mind and heart, that I have you at home in my place this blessed Christmas.

I am certain as well that your mother is happy also and it is my prayer that you will remember for ever the care and attention

that your dearest mother is giving to you in your youth, when
you are not able to do anything
for yourself.

    With greatest love to your
mother and to ye all.

From your Father

> 22 : XII : 16
>
> Do Tomás Óg Mac Curtáin —
>
> A leinbh mo chroidhe
> Tá athas ar mo chroidhe air
> ar m'aigne, tusa do bheith agam
> sa bhaile im' meadh-sa an
> Nodlaig beannuighthe-seo.
> Táim deimhnightheach, cómh maith
> go bhfuil an t-athair ceadna
> air do mháthair agus ró mo
> shuidhe go scuimhneochair go deo
> air an scuram agus an oidhche
> dhá as do mháthair dílis 'a
> tabhairt duit anois 'e' oidhche
> nuair ná fuil ar do chumas
> aon rud a dheanamh duit féin
> le grádh mo chroidhe dot'
> mháthair agus díbh go léir
> ó t'athair.

Tomás knew that his absence
made life very difficult at
home and he realised that the
women of Ireland were really
the backbone of any organi-
sation. It was left to them to keep the home
fires burning, make ends meet and raise the children in the absence of their men folk. His brother Seán, who had managed to
visit him in Reading a few times, had been released some time
earlier and was keeping the business ticking over – but the mill
and shop were just about surviving.

    Even though Tomás was in jail the house was being raided
on a regular basis. Elizabeth never mentioned this in her letters
but he always found out. Some of the lads who were 'in' with
him would get letters and a 'disruptive visit' to the Mac Curtáins
would be mentioned.

The British government declared an amnesty before Christmas
1916 and many Volunteers were allowed to return home. Christmas week came but Tomás was not granted release or Christmas
parole. Elizabeth and the children had come to terms with the fact

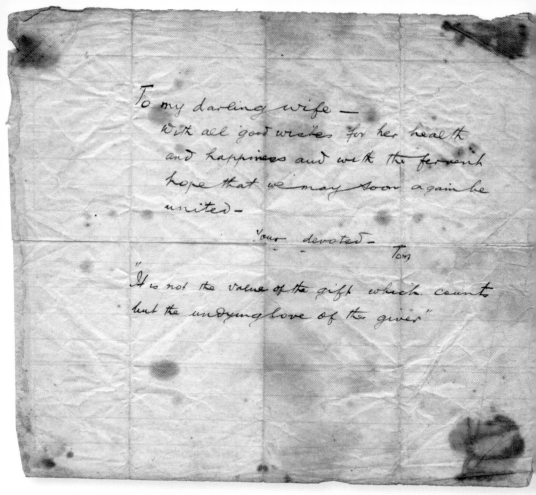

To my darling wife —
With all good wishes for her health
and happiness and with the fervent
hope that we may soon again be
united —

Your devoted —
Tom

"It is not the value of the gift which counts
but the undying love of the giver"

NOTE SENT BY TOMÁS TO EILÍS: 'IT IS NOT THE VALUE OF THE GIFT WHICH COUNTS BUT THE UNDYING LOVE OF THE GIVER'

that he would not get home for Christmas even though she had been hopeful. As the clock struck midnight on 24 December and as she climbed the stairs to retire, there were tears in her eyes. The children had all been asking, 'Would dada be home?' All week long she had said maybe, but tonight as they went to bed, she had been honest and said, 'No my darlings, not this Christmas, maybe the New Year. He sends his love and he knows that we are all thinking of him.'

Christmas morning dawned and the excitement was at fever pitch around the house. Elizabeth had insisted that they would all go to mass before the presents were exchanged. Just after noon, the gifts were unwrapped and they all sat down to a meal together. Later they sat around the table and chatted until Elizabeth, her mum, two brothers Tommy and Jimmy, Hannah and the children were all tired. (The two Walsh sisters, Annie and Susie, were in Spain teaching.) Elizabeth smiled to herself. All in all things had gone well. They had enough money for small gifts for everybody and the children had had a great day. She re-read the prayer that Tomás had sent her and his note. He never missed an opportunity to tell her he loved her.

The commotion at the door startled her. Jimmy went down to see what was happening. A group of excited Volunteers were outside and she reacted to the shouts of 'Mrs Mac, you better come down, Mrs Mac where are you …' Elizabeth hurried to the open door. Tomás emerged from the crowd of men. She felt as if her heart had missed a beat as she ran towards his open arms. The loneliness, sadness and sorrow ebbed away as she felt the comfort of his embrace.

Tomás fell into the chair with exhaustion from the journey and the children threw themselves on top of him with happiness. He told them the British authorities had granted him release on 24 December. A day and a half later, he was here, home with his family. His heart ached with love and pride. Elizabeth's smile was always with him.

After his release, the topic of the Rising came up with many Volunteers and none of them blamed Tomás for his actions at the time. It was clear that he had no alternatives. The movement seemed dead to observers, but the true believers were still in constant contact.

Seán Curtin was finding himself run ragged, not that he complained. He was a shareholder in the mill but still retained the existing business on Shandon Street in a large premises spreading across 52, 53 and 54. That shop traded under the name of Curtin Bros. Tomás and he had come to an arrangement that Seán would own Shandon Street and he, in turn, would now have sole responsibility for the mill.

Life in Thomas Davis Street settled down once again. Business was not good and the mill was just about surviving. When the grain was delivered to the docks, the bags were constantly slashed with bayonets and the sacks were so damaged that many times there was less than half the contents left in them by the time Tomás took the delivery. There was very little spare money around. Many of the households had their men folk away in the war and were subsidising their income with part time jobs. The Artan clothing factory employed many locals and the sale of clothes was steady but small. It was difficult for Tomás to adapt, having been in the company of men for so long. Elizabeth and the children got used to having him around. There was never peace and tranquillity, but Elizabeth was happy to have him home and by now was used to the turmoil of raids, as they had become part of her daily life.

Tomás and Elizabeth had time to talk and make decisions on various issues including having the children taught by the Mac-Swiney sisters. The accounts for the mill had to be checked and updated. Tomás liked to cast an eye over the orders, deliveries and the outstanding payments so the ledgers were piled up in front of him. It hit him again the amount of work that Elizabeth had to do on a daily basis and he felt guilty about leaving her to cope

40 Thomas Davis St
February 4/1917

Dear Miss McSweeney —

Many thanks for your very kind and thoughtful offer to us re children. We had decided to send them to you, as undoubtedly they couldn't attend a more suitable place. We hope to be able to send them up during the week.

...desired me to express to you her gratitude for your kindness and hopes the children will not be too troublesome to you.

Mise le meas mór
ᵃ̇ racḃ-ḃe uᵹᵘᵖ aᵖ.
ḃuƿ n-aḃuƿ. ——

Tomás Mac Curtáin
——

with so much. However, he knew that she was happy to do her bit and she would have it no other way. Where would he be without her? He knew the best day of his life was when Elizabeth agreed to marry him.

Tomás' freedom and pleasures of home life were not to last long and on the 26 February District Inspector Swanzy arrested him. He was brought to Kings Street barracks first. Terence was then arrested and both were transferred to the military detention barracks where Seán Nolan and Peadar O'Hourihane were being held. Tomás asked to see his solicitor on his first night in jail and made the new verbal working agreement with Seán legal. It had weighed heavily on his mind that if something happened to him or if he was away for a long time all his affairs would not be in order. Now his mind was at ease, at least in that regard and Seán could now devote his full time to his own business.

Tomás was taken with Peadar and Terry Mac to Arbour Hill. This time, after various stops, he was sent to Ledbury and Terry Mac was sent to Bromyard. Though not surrounded by prison walls this type of exile was very difficult. Yes, it was easier than prison but there was a terrible emptiness. It was like a house arrest. They were not locked up but they were confined to certain areas of England and the English government would not give them any type of living allowance. How they survived was in their own hands. There was no chance of even getting a part time job. The women at home were financially stretched as it was and now had an extra strain of trying to send money to give their loved ones the most basic of essentials. Eventually, in mid March the British government gave in to pressure from the prisoners and their families and agreed to pay for board and lodgings.

If they left the small area where they were confined, they would

Tomás and Seán Nolan (lady unknown)
at Malvern Hills, England, Summer 1917

be arrested and incarcerated. Tomás missed his family terribly and spent much of his time writing to Elizabeth. Yet he also enjoyed many hours talking to the parish priest Fr O'Keeffe, smoking his pipe and playing music. Fr O'Keeffe had acquired an old violin and saw the delight and pleasure on Tomás' face when he lent it to him. Letters from Ireland went to a café and Tomás made an arrangement with the owner that he would call every day to see if there was any post. He did not want it sent to the house where he was staying in case he was suddenly moved and his letters would go astray. He loved the prospect of going in for a cup of tea with the hope of some post to read. When mail arrived, he would sit with his cuppa, his pipe and read, reread and devour every morsel of news and gossip. The letters kept him going for days and then the prospect of another letter helped keep his spirits up.

Seán and Elizabeth wrote often and he was delighted with Siobhán's little notes. He knew the effort that went into them and he tried to write back sounding cheerful, and trying to give the impression to the children that it was like a holiday. He did not pretend to Elizabeth and it was very difficult to make his letters sound light-hearted as he knew that Elizabeth would not be fooled. She was very aware of what her husband was going through. Each saw in the other a soul partner and had an inner contentment in spite of the separations.

Tomás did not find the days too long if he had his music and poetry. He awoke on Easter Monday and the first anniversary of the Rising was like a winter's day. The wind howled and he could see his breath hanging like smoke in the cold air. He was sure it was going to snow and felt the atmosphere suited his mood. The limit of Tomás' enforced boundary of travel was Bromyard so he met up with Terry Mac and Seán Nolan there and they mulled over the events of Easter 1916 again and again. They all agreed that nothing else could have been done in Cork, but it was a bitter pill to swallow. He prayed fervently for the souls of his executed comrades that weekend and wrote to Elizabeth and the children.

The amount of time he was spending away from his family was depressing him. He hardly knew his young son. Tomás had been born in 1915 and after the death of his first son, Patrick, the birth of another boy was special. They loved their two girls, yet another son was an extra blessing for himself and Elizabeth. This baby was too young to even know that when Tomás kissed him goodbye the night of his arrest it would be months before he would see him again. Siobhán, his eldest daughter on the other hand fully understood the implications of Dada being taken away.

Tomás kissed him goodbye the night of his arrest it would be months before he would see him again.

Later in the month, Terry came to visit him and told him that he and Muriel were going to marry in June. Muriel came from Cork and was one of the Murphys, the owners of the brewery in Cork. Although they had no idea when they would be released the couple had decided to set the date anyway. Tomás was thrilled with the good news and they all looked forward to the wedding.

The eyes of the world were beginning to focus a little on Ireland. There had been keen interest in the Rising and the British government's actions had not placated the feelings of uneasiness coming from overseas. Lloyd George, the British prime minister, set up an inquiry to put together a report on how to proceed in

Ireland. This eventually led to a recommendation that the Irish MPs attend the house of commons, but the nationalist view was never considered. The tide of public opinion had changed and the British forces were now under pressure to treat the Irish fairly. A strong following for 'the cause' was growing in the United States as many patriots, who had either gone on the run or were exiled, had moved to the United States and were gaining support there and were being joined by exiles on almost a daily basis. This American support would prove vital in the years ahead.

Elizabeth's family came to a decision that they would leave the family home at Moorfield Terrace and all move into Thomas Davis Street. There was so much empty accommodation it seemed the most practical step. Elizabeth's mother needed care, and at the same time her sister and brother wanted, and needed to, spend time with Elizabeth and help her to mind the children as she was expecting another child. She had not known when Tomás was arrested in February and had hoped that he would be home soon so she could tell him. She had delayed for months in the hope that she would not need to write, but well … now he knew.

Her brothers and sisters felt that a new baby, Mary's children and her own were just too much for anybody to be expected to cope with, more especially with Tomás away. There was ample room for them on the top floor of the house attached to the mill and the new arrangement worked well for them all. Tomás was relieved as he knew that Eilís was nervous in the house by night. This certainly seemed the perfect answer.

He wrote to Elizabeth:

24 May 1917

… We have them in a corner now, Eilís and only simplicity,

foolishness and perhaps deceit will make us let them down easy. However, God is on the side of right and we are going to come out on the top this time.

Are you well, I hope so. Hope you aren't working too hard and for goodness sake Lizzie don't worry. I heard you say you are proud you had a brother in the fight, do consider me as in it also and won't I be happy if I feel that you are proud of my efforts on behalf of my country.

My forefather and yours, thank God, stood for Ireland and were hunted, some of them from their homes, for their fidelity. We are today proud of their sacrifices and honour their memory. We are only too glad to follow in their footsteps. The path of right and duty is always a difficult and hard one, but there is a pleasure in feeling that you have helped in the great work, that you have done as those who came before you and not disgraced their memory. This generation vindicates the principles of Tone and brings within realisation the writings of Emmet's epitaph. I am certain, Lizzie that we will see the dream of centuries realised and the ideal for which Irish men and women have shed rivers of blood become an actual fact.

May God grant it, but if in his wisdom the goal is not yet near, then thank God that this generation has upheld the honour of our century and can hand on to the next the cause and fight unsullied by dishonour and shame. We are prouder than ever of being Irish. 'Tis Empire Day here and there is nothing but Union Jacks and a big meeting in the square here. Seán and I walked through with our heads in the air ignoring their flags and their Empire and let them plainly understand our feeling by our attitude. We want no connection with this rotten empire …

Opinions. We have them in a corner now Eilís and only simplicity, foolishness and perhaps deceit will make us let them down easy. However God is on the side Of right and we are going to come out on top this time —

Are you all well, I hope so. I hope you aren't working too hard and for goodness sake Lizzie Don't worry. I heard You say you were proud You had a brother in the fight do consider me as in it also and won't I be happy if I feel that You are proud of my efforts on behalf of my country.

My fore fathers and yours thank God — stood for Ireland and were hunted Some of them from their homes for their fidelity, we are to-day proud of their Sacrifices and honour their memory, we are only too glad to follow in their footsteps; the path of right and duty is always a difficult and hard one, but there is a pleasure in feeling that you have keeped in the great work, that you

EXTRACT FROM A LETTER TOMÁS SENT TO EILÍS 24 MAY 1917

His letter ended: 'Our own we want, our own we'll have, but we covet not our neighbour's property.'

Life in Ireland had totally altered for Sinn Féin since the Easter Rising. There was now an enormous ground-swell of support, but without a clearly defined political party machine behind it. A vacancy arose in Roscommon and Count Plunkett stood and was elected in a landslide victory. One of his son's had signed the proclamation and had been executed; his other sons were in jail and he had suffered as he had been ostracised by many people and was fired from his job as a director of the Science and Art Museum. Tomás and Lizzie watched the events with interest and were glad the Volunteers had gained strength in its numbers in Cork but upset that the British took possession of the hall in Sheares Street early in June and closed it down.

10

Home and the Future

Many of the prisoner's sentences were reduced and on 21 June Tomás walked down Thomas Davis Street. He was five days late for Tomás Óg's birthday but not to worry, he was home. It took him less than an hour to see for himself that the British forces had occupied the Volunteers' Hall in Sheares Street.

There was a new-found interest in all things Irish – old songs became popular and there was a great demand for books and historical articles. After the leaders of the Rising had been executed there was a keen interest in the speeches Pearse had made. The idea of a Republic became a commonplace topic of conversation. After his return Tomás and Elizabeth discussed endlessly the best ways to capitalise on this new wave of interest.

Many activists decided the way forward was to stand for election. Count Plunkett had a great win but immediately declared that he would not take up his seat in the British parliament as he would be standing for a free Ireland. A volunteer officer Éamon de Valera had another great victory in the Clare elections. Victory after victory for the Republicans took place. The voice of the people was gaining strength and it was only because of the public outcry that Thomas Ashe had not been executed for his part in the 1916 Rising. His poem, 'Let me carry your cross for Ireland, Lord' was being read all over Ireland. He had been released during the summer of 1917 only to be rearrested and sentenced at a court martial. Ashe went on hunger strike for political status and while the authorities were trying to force feed him, the tube they inserted perforated his lung and he died on 25 September. His hunger strike once again brought world attention to the Irish fight for freedom. Tomás led a commemoration parade with battalions of the Volunteers and led the prayers at the National Monument. Once again, one of his comrades had paid the ultimate price but the struggle would continue.

The British government prohibited any outward display by the Volunteers or, for that matter, by any body of men. Carrying arms, the wearing of uniforms or any such action was forbidden. The first nationwide challenge to this ban took place on Sunday 21 October. In Cork, approximately 1,000 volunteers met outside the closed hall at Sheares Street and marched to Blarney. Tomás led the parade and Terence marched with him; both men wore uniforms and were followed by their men. Most did not have uniforms but used any bits and pieces they possessed: some had caps, others belts, others only boots. They marched, but no arms were on display. Tomás was in no doubt as to what the outcome would be for leading the men in the march. 'We knew we would be arrested, but something new was needed to raise the spirit of

Tomás' arrest card, October 1917

the people.' He was arrested and held for a short time in Cork Prison.

A Volunteer convention was held soon after this. Tomás attended in Dublin and saw the election of Éamon de Valera as president and Cathal Brugha as chief of staff. The following day the Sinn Féin Convention was held in the Mansion House.

When he returned home he told Elizabeth all about the new developments but he was only home for one day when he was arrested with a number of other men. When brought before the court, Tomás spoke in Irish and said, 'I have not the slightest respect for this foreign court. Its ruling I will not follow, its laws I will not accept, and furthermore I will not speak its language. I will be true to the ideals of the men who established the Republic last Easter. From their deaths will come the freedom of the land of Ireland.' Each prisoner said the same thing. The judge was outraged at this display of defiance and sentenced each man to six months in jail. Tomás was back in jail and did what he did best – he organised the men and took the opportunity to build stronger bonds.

Christmas 1917 saw him released and back with Elizabeth and the children. The executives of Sinn Féin asked him to stand for election in South Armagh just after the new year. Tomás and Elizabeth discussed the implications of this offer, including his absence and its consequences. They decided he would travel north and he asked any Volunteers who were available to come up and assist him. Sinn Féin did not win but Tomás was delighted with the heightened profile of the party and the Volunteer movement.

In March many of the leaders were arrested again. Tomás knew it was only a matter of time before he would be re-arrested so he went on the run. This meant he had to be away from Elizabeth and the children and even though his business would suffer he was determined to put the time to good use. He visited the battalions of Volunteers all over Cork county as he wanted them to be a disciplined and well-trained force. He instilled into the men once again the necessity of obeying orders. On 9 April, Lloyd George declared that the conscription bill under debate in England would apply to Ireland and the Irish Party withdrew from the British House of Commons. A meeting was held in the Mansion House on 18 April and declared that the British government had no right to enforce conscription. Conscription would be resisted by whatever means necessary as the young men who would be conscripted were now the backbone of the Volunteer force. Lord French laid out his plans and stated that if he did not get 50,000 men by 1 October and 20,000 each month thereafter

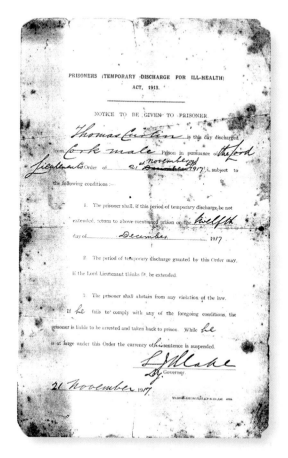

he would enforce conscription. He failed to reach his stated target and the Volunteers maintained that they would resist conscription by military force, if necessary.

The police raided 40 Thomas Davis Street on a regular basis looking for Tomás. Elizabeth assured him that there was no need to worry. She and the children were doing fine and he was to stay away from the house as it was being watched by the authorities waiting for his return. They had no trouble in sending messages back and forth as a network of Volunteers cycled from house to house. When one was tired another took over and this system covered the whole county. Tomás' time was spent dodging arrest and going from safe house to safe house. During this time, he held a firm grip on the movement and controlled it from wherever he was. He was pleased with the organisation and with the development of the men.

Tomás went home for a quick visit during Christmas 1918 and by January it appeared that the RIC were easing the pressure on Volunteer leaders so he returned home to live but he always kept one eye on the door in case he was in danger of being arrested. Action was stepped up in early January. GHQ sanctioned attacks on RIC barracks to acquire arms. Cork No. 1 brigade was the first to capture an RIC barracks in Carrigtwohill, County Cork and building on this success the Volunteers continued to target other barracks. January also saw the necessity of reorganising the Volunteer movement. Tomás' territory was now too vast to manage because of the number of men involved and because it consisted of the territory from beyond Ballyvourney to the city. He was constantly travelling but tried to get home as often as possible, or to meet with Elizabeth and the children in safe houses. Michael Collins came down from HQ in Dublin to consult with him.

The British were sending in reinforcements and these soon started flowing into Ireland. It was decided that Tomás would stand for the corporation election in Cork as he was a very public figure, known for his various business interests in Cork and his involvement with the Volunteers. He saw this as the next move he had to make – not as an individual but as a commander of the Irish Volunteer force.

The British were losing their grip on the rural areas but they would most definitely make a stand to hold onto the cities. Tomás felt that as the commander of his men he should stand up and be counted. This decision made the road ahead even more fraught with danger.

11

Municipal Elections in Cork

E lizabeth never doubted the outcome of the election for one moment: Tomás topped the poll in Cork ward north-west three. Sinn Féin did well all round and their vote would ultimately select the Lord Mayor. The 30 January dawned and the Lord Mayor was to be elected. Con Harrington had told Tomás that he was the Sinn Féin candidate for the position but Tomás feared what might be ahead as he had been told and given an anonymous written warning, that if he took up the position of Lord Mayor he would be killed. He was, after all, the commander of Cork's No. 1 brigade of the Volunteers and was leading an armed struggle against the British establishment in the area. He felt he had no choice – it was his duty as a soldier.

He had sneaked into his rooms at the city hall at 7.00 a.m. to make sure he avoided arrest. Some of the members of Sinn Féin could not be there: Fred Murray was in jail awaiting trial and J. J.

| CANDIDATES | RESULT OF EACH COUNT | | | | | | | ELECTED |
	1st	2nd	3rd	4th	5th	6th	7th	
BYRNE	203	224	225	232	234	237	275	BYRNE (3)
EGAN	121	130	137	153	170	190	197	EGAN (6)
FORDE	76	149	188	221	228	230	260	FORDE (5)
GERAN	23	28	35	44	45	-	-	
HODART	25	26	28	35	37	-	-	
KELLEHER	4	5	-	-	-	-	-	
LUCEY	245	443	-	-	-	-	-	LUCEY (2)
LYONS	66	68	73	81	93	98	99	
MAC CURTAIN	765	-	-	-	-	-	-	MAC CURTAIN (1
McAULEY	106	118	124	134	155	188	191	
MACK	3	-	-	-	-	-	-	
O'CONNELL	12	13	14	-	-	-	-	
O'LEARY	69	77	78	79	85	-	-	
O'QUILL	52	163	246	248	254	282	367	O'QUILL (4)
QUINLAN	40	108	141	151	169	172	-	
WALSH	16	19	19	19	20	-	-	
WHELAN	32	33	33	-	-	-	-	

Walsh, a good friend of Tomás', was on the run. When the members sat down to elect the Mayor, fifty-one answered the roll call and of the fifty-six names listed, forty were staunch Sinn Féiners. The proceedings were conducted in Irish and they took great pride in answering 'anseo'. Micheál Ó Cuill proposed Tomás and Terry Mac seconded him. He was unanimously elected and he accepted the position of first Republican Lord Mayor of Cork.

Bedlam surrounded the investiture. Elizabeth and her brother Jimmy were there and they thought they would burst with pride. All Elizabeth could think of was that the love of her life was standing there, the first citizen of their city. They had dreamed of making a difference and here he was not ten feet away from her with the Mayoral chain around his neck. She had seen the passion to serve that ran in Tomás' veins. The trappings that went with the Mayoral office meant nothing to him but he recognised and welcomed the doors it would open for him to further the cause of freedom – universal recognition of a free Ireland was his main focus.

Elizabeth was immensely proud of his speech – he spoke of his desire for 'a nation once again' but cautioned that just because

The last known Mac Curtáin family picture

CORPORATION MEMBERS IN COUNCIL CHAMBERS THE NIGHT TOMÁS WAS ELECTED

the past administration was old this did not mean it was all bad. He vowed to carefully consider the way forward, nothing at this point should be rushed, everything should be evaluated. Cast off what was bad, retain and build on what was good. He made it clear that he saw his acceptance of this office more as a soldier, stepping into the breach, than as an administrator fulfilling the first post of the municipality. Under his privilege as Lord Mayor, he brought a special matter before the council. He asked that a resolution be proposed pledging the council's allegiance to Dáil Éireann. Up to this point, the Lord Mayor reported to the British local government department. His proposal was moved by Alderman Liam de Róiste and seconded by Terry Mac and the resolution was passed. Tomás stood proud and honoured, wearing a Sinn Féin rosette that had been presented to him by a member of Cumann na mBan.

For the first time the tricolour was hoisted over the City Hall. A new beginning had dawned. It was proposed that a substantial increase should be made to the salary of the Lord Mayor and the sum of £1,000 was put forward. Tomás objected because he believed the

citizens of Cork were in no position to pay this type of money and there were too many people hungry in the city as it was.

Very few speeches were made and Tomás said they were there to work and could do without the froth. It had been an old custom that the Lord Mayor could choose his spiritual advisor, so he appointed Fr Dominic as his chaplain. Fr Dominic had been chaplain to the Cork Volunteers and a great confidant of Tomás. He said he had done much soul searching and assured the Volunteers that theirs was a just cause and therefore under the flag of Ireland some activities that would normally be unacceptable were justified. He was close to a great number of the Volunteers and some of them received the sacraments from him.

Elizabeth was aware that Tomás did not approve of many of the actions that the IRB were taking and realised it was a very difficult time for him because his opinion of legitimate targets and that of the IRB leaders differed. He was commander of the Irish Volunteers and would stand over his orders. As Lord Mayor he was an elected member of Sinn Féin with a mandate to serve his city.

12

St Patrick's Weekend – 1920

What a great weekend they all had! The Agriculture Show had been on and Tomás had made an official visit. Elizabeth, the children and Jimmy had gone with him. The Ford Motor Company had opened in Cork in 1919 and had brought great employment to the area. The factory was located on the opposite side of the river to Blackpool and near the mouth of the estuary. The girls loved seeing their dad driving the Ford tractor as part of a demonstration and there were squeals of delight as Tomás headed off to plough a part of the track. His training as a boy on the farms in Ballyknockane stood him well. Numerous photographs were taken; the pipe band had played and there was a festive atmosphere. Tomás had to stay there for hours, as everybody wanted to shake hands with the new Lord Mayor – where he found his energy, nobody knew. The family returned to Thomas Davis Street exhausted, but happy.

THE LAST KNOWN PHOTO OF TOMÁS, DRIVING THE NEW FORD TRACTOR

On the night of 19 March, Elizabeth was bone weary but she knew it was worse for Tomás. It seemed like weeks since he had had a good night's sleep and she hoped he would be able to rest in the morning. His birthday the next day was to be a special day with their children and his in-laws, who he felt were like brothers and sisters. They showered all members of the household with unconditional love. Everybody was excited by the prospect of the small surprise party that was planned. The cake was made and hidden. There were gifts: the children had found fun trinkets for him; Annie, Susie and Hannah, Elizabeth's sisters, bought him books and she herself had purchased a silver match holder. He still enjoyed smoking his pipe on rare occasions. Tomás had promised to take the day easy, but she knew him better than that. Something was bound to come up so she had planned the party for lunchtime.

Everybody had settled down for the night. Elizabeth's mother on the top floor was sound asleep, the children were in bed, and all was quiet. Elizabeth went up to bed at about 8.30 p.m. She did not sleep, just rested and waited for Tomás to come home. He had stopped off at Sheares Street and was late – but that was nothing new. He had spent a considerable time on the phone to the hospital checking the condition of a policeman, Murtagh, who had been shot earlier in the night. Tomás hoped that there would be no further disruption in the city that night. Many police had been shot over the last few months and this had put Tomás' life in jeopardy as he had been warned that if actions between the Volunteers and the RIC became worse, his own life would be in danger. He had received so many warnings that he was going to be killed that they were by now nearly part of his daily routine. The news was grave and Tomás made sure to contact the Murtagh family to pass on his condolences. He had not told Elizabeth of the new threat he had heard.

When he arrived home Tomás spent a long time getting ready for bed and stood at the window longer than usual. It was now a ritual: the gas worker cowling the city lights would pass below the Lord Mayor's window and give him the signal that all was well. He was a little later than usual and Tomás waited but once he saw the nod and wave, he went to bed. They were unaware that in the streets of Cork men in plain clothes and uniformed police were now turning back lamplighters and others who were approaching Blackpool. The area in and around the Lord Mayor's house was being isolated.

It seemed to Elizabeth that she had just closed her eyes when a loud banging on the door woke her. She reacted quickly and got out of bed, warning Tomás to stay where he was. Hurrying to the window, she lifted it a little to ask who was there and what was the matter. The cold March air chilled her and she pulled her shawl tightly across her frozen shoulders. A loud voice shouted from below, 'Come down' and then repeated it more urgently and loudly. Elizabeth hurriedly put on her dressing-gown and because of her pregnancy, was slower than usual moving from the bed to the door and onto the landing. Tomás was out of their bed, pulling his trousers on and making his way to the bedroom door to answer the caller. 'I'll go myself,' he mumbled.

Elizabeth would have none of it. She was out the door before him and down the stairs. She descended the stairs with a sense of apprehension wondering what could be so urgent that the Lord Mayor would be called at one o'clock in the morning. As she reached the door, shattered glass flew towards her and the front door was almost broken down. She pulled the latch towards her. A man with a blackened face hurled himself toward the stairs shouting, 'Where is Mac Curtain?'

> Strange rough hands grabbed Elizabeth. The blackened-faced armed strangers rushed passed her up the stairs.

Elizabeth answered, 'Upstairs'.

More men with rifles followed in behind, looking at the woman in the hall. A commanding voice ordered, 'Hold that one'. Six men in total had now come through the doorway.

Strange rough hands grabbed Elizabeth. The blackened-faced and armed strangers rushed passed her up the stairs. They seemed to know exactly where they were going. They stopped on the first landing at the door of the Lord Mayor's room. Annie and Susie had heard the commotion on the floor beneath their room and had come down. Susie was frantically screaming for her brother who had retired earlier. 'Jimmy, Jimmy!' the hysterical cry could be heard. Jimmy pulled on his clothes and put his pipe in his pocket, thinking that he was about to be arrested. He arrived at the door of his room just in time to hear the shout, 'Come out Mac Curtain we want you.' He saw two tall men, one of whom wore a light overcoat facing the bedroom. The baby Eilís was in the main bedroom, howling. Susie pushed her way past the frightening blackened faces to pick up and console the crying infant but was ordered back out of the way. 'Please,' she begged, 'let me take the baby.' But her requests were ignored. They were stopped just at the entrance to the main landing from their rooms on the next floor.

They heard the gun shots and saw the backs of the men as they left the house.

Tomás was at the door. Jimmy was silent and had a sideways view of the group. He staggered in shock as the sound of the shot from the revolver rang out. A second shot followed. As the bullets were fired, the baby stopped crying. Jimmy blew out the candle, as he had not been spotted. He was powerless. He was unarmed and there was nothing he could do. The perpetrators had guns drawn less than ten feet away from him. He crouched down on the stairs. The men turned to go down stairs and Jimmy spotted the children. He darted across the landing and motioned the children to lie flat on the floor. He rushed to the bedroom window and shouted for help. When Susie had shouted for her brother, Tomás Óg and Siobhán had heard the commotion and they were peeping through the keyhole when the shots were fired.

They were on the landing before anybody could get to the Lord Mayor. A mixture of screaming and shouting could be heard as Elizabeth tried to get up the stairs. Some of the perpetrators rushing to leave the house bundled Elizabeth from the end of the stairs out into the street and she was frantic to get back inside. She could hear her brother Jimmy shouting out the upstairs window. The order 'fire' came from behind her, ordering the group at the door of the main shop to shoot. They pointed their weapons at Jimmy and showered the window area with bullets.

Inside the house, there was total chaos. Elizabeth's sisters, Anne and Susie, heard the shots and saw the backs of the men as they left the house. Jimmy had come back in from the window and went straight to his brother-in-law. Tomás was slowly sliding down the landing wall. A trail of blood was left on the wall behind him. Jimmy struck a match and the blood glistened in its light. He heard an almost inaudible moan, 'The children Jim.'

> A trail of blood was left on the wall behind him. Jimmy struck a match and the blood glistened in its light.

'You're only wounded boy', Jimmy said to Tomás, and by this time the children were at their father's side.

Outside the assassins marched away from the scene of their destruction.

Elizabeth instinctively had known, even before Jimmy had shouted, that they had shot Tomás. She screamed at the crowd for somebody to get the priest. Peg Duggan and her sister, who were neighbours, took off running towards the North Cathedral.

Elizabeth rushed back up the stairs. She stopped at the top of the landing. Everything seemed to be moving in slow motion.

Tomás' bloodied body lay on the floor. Her sister Annie had her right arm under his head. Tomás Óg rushed towards her: 'Mama they have shot Dada', he said.

For a moment, there was utter silence. 'Oh God,' thought Elizabeth, 'have they shot the baby too?' There was absolutely no sound coming from the pram.

Suddenly the crying started again, as if the baby had only paused to regain her strength.

Elizabeth's mind refocused and she knew instantly that things looked very bad. 'Help, get a doctor, quickly. Where is the priest?' she barked the order.

The exchange put her through to the doctor. She quickly explained that Tomás had been shot and that she thought he was dying. She dropped to her knees and the tears poured down her face.

Annie looked up at Elizabeth. 'Sacred Heart, spare him' she said, bowing her head, and praying that he might last, at least until the priest arrived. Annie relinquished her place beside Tomás to allow her sister to tend to her dying husband. Blood from the wound oozed through his white nightshirt. Tomás Óg had edged his way between the wall and his father's back and was half holding his father's head. The warm blood that had come from his father's body and trailed down the wall stuck to his hand. It had a warm clammy feeling.

Annie ran to the bedroom and found his crucifix and his little prayer book, *The Imitation of Christ*. Hannah's loving arms encircled Síle, who sobbed 'Dada'. There was no comforting the child.

Fr Butts from the North Cathedral pushed through the crowd that had gathered on the street outside the door of the shop. A path was made for him. He rushed upstairs to administer the last sacraments.

The children were now hysterical. Síle's sobbing was getting louder and louder. Máire wept as the adults were torn between making soothing sounds to the dying man and attempting to calm the frightened, exhausted children. Through all this time Eilís, the baby in the pram near the bed, screamed and screamed and no amount of comforting would stop her high-pitched screaming. It was a house of uproar. Tomás was alive but only just. He was murmuring words to his young son and expressions of love and prayers to his family.

All present knew that these had been fatal shots.

The family surrounded him and said imploring prayers for Tomás to be saved but it was futile. Elizabeth and her sisters had tried to shield the children. Watching their father, his life's blood oozing through his nightshirt, it was no place for them yet they had a right to spend these last few minutes with their father. Tomás knew they were there and this was very important to everyone.

People started rushing back and forth in the streets, as word spread; the Lord Mayor had been shot.

The gunshots appeared to have entered close to his heart and blood was now seeping freely through his nightshirt. Tomás Óg contin-

'Into Thy hands O Lord, I commend my spirit.'

ued to kneel, in the corner, by the slumped body and cradle his father's head. The Lord Mayor, first citizen of Cork, opened his eyes and looked up. He appeared to focus a little over the heads of his family and said 'Into Thy hands O Lord, I commend my spirit.' Then there was complete silence. The children were like statues. Síle was in shock in Hannah's arms and did not stir. No noise came from the crowd in the street. The priest continued his prayers, but made no sound – only his lips moved.

Tomás looked into Elizabeth's eyes, his beloved Elizabeth. They did not have to declare their love, it was obvious. They had always seemed to share a single heart.

Showing her character and strength she leaned forward and said, 'Remember darling it's all for Ireland.' There followed what seemed an endless silence, as if time and the world stood still.

The fear of the impending disaster was almost tangible.

In fact, it took only a few minutes. Tomás sighed and closed his eyes. His breathing became quieter and it seemed to take a longer time between the intakes of his laboured breathing. He then took a deep breath, almost a gasp for air and it rattled slowly out of his body. It was his last breath.

'Remember darling, it's all for Ireland.'

The family could hear Doctor O'Connor rushing up the stairs and stood back. Elizabeth moved to her husband's side allowing the doctor the necessary space to examine him. He pronounced what everyone was dreading. Tomás was dead.

The stunned group knelt by the corpse in silent shock. They were immobile. It was almost impossible to comprehend.

Tomás Mac Curtáin, first Republican Lord Mayor of Cork, had been shot dead by the RIC. Two bullets had been fired less than three yards from his body. One broke his ribs with the impact and remained lodged. The other tore through his heart, ripped through his body and was lodged in the wall behind him. A murder, a shocking act, in the dead of night, committed in front of his pregnant wife and young children.

13

The Lord Mayor is Dead

The spell-like atmosphere broke. Elizabeth started to react. 'Help me lift him to the bed,' she asked her grief-stricken family. They all helped to carry the bloodied body onto the bed that was still warm, even the children. Elizabeth pulled her thoughts together and began issuing instructions. 'Annie, mind the children. Susie, check on Mama, Jimmy ...'

The body was cleaned and laid out by Elizabeth. It looked like a hospital bed. Clean white starched sheets, stiff and crisp were folded back. Tomás looked at peace. The family began their night vigil of prayers.

Elizabeth comforted baby Eilís in her arms and went downstairs with Fr Butts to see him out. He delayed in the shop still consoling the newly widowed mother.

A banging on the front door interrupted them.

'Excuse me,' Elizabeth said turning to answer the door with the child in her arms.

'Police, Mam,' a voice announced.

'Are you going to kill my brother now?' asked Elizabeth

'We have come to arrest Tomás Mac Curtáin and we have a warrant to search the premises.'

'My husband has just been shot and is dead.'

They pushed past her.

By this time, Jimmy was halfway down the stairs. Three bayonets were put against his body. He asked what they wanted and in his heart of hearts he really thought they had come back to shoot him. They prodded him up the stairs. His hands could barely hold the candle steady. They again said they were going to 'search the whole house'. Jimmy asked where they would like to search first.

'Surely there is no need for you to still search,' Elizabeth said as the men passed by her into the house.

'Orders, Mam,' was the gruff reply, as Elizabeth put the infant back in her pram.

The team searched the house systematically room by room. When they approached the main bedroom Elizabeth again interrupted them.

'Don't you understand? My husband is lying in there, he has been shot and is dead. My family are at the bedside praying!'

She tried to continue protesting, but in vain. She was talking to their backs as they brushed past her, passed her young children who were in deep shock. Ignored, her eyes full of tears, Elizabeth stood and watched.

The search continued. The police pulled up the mattress to look underneath. The still warm body of the Lord Mayor was tossed to the floor. Annie and Susie stood back in utter shock and horror. The baby wailed in her pram.

They raiders went from room to room, slashing mattresses and destroying the family's belongings. They even searched the children's area and Elizabeth's mother's bed.

The police found nothing and eventually left. Later it transpired that the only documents or weapons in the house was Tomás' personal revolver, hidden under the mattress in the baby Eilís' pram.

Elizabeth's face was waxen and harrowed with grief. She looked around her trying to understand what had taken place. Far too much had happened so fast and now there was a deathly silence. Less than two hours earlier he had been looking out the window and she lay in bed talking to him. Now he was dead.

Her children and family were distraught – Siobhán and Tomás Óg were the worst at this moment. They had witnessed part of the murder. Siobhán's hands shook as if she had palsy and her legs kept going in a rhythmic convulsion, like the regular beating of a drum. During the time their father lay there dying, she had stared in almost total silence. It was if she had taken every breath with him.

Elizabeth gathered the children to her. The morning of his thirty-sixth birthday dawned as Tomás was again laid out on the bed which he and Elizabeth had shared, close to the window.

Unopened birthday gifts lay downstairs. The special birthday cake, with candles that would never be lit, lay uncut.

The man who was to be celebrated was gone. His birthday party would now be his wake.

> Elizabeth's face was waxen and harrowed with grief. She looked around her trying to understand what had taken place.

'Dada is gone to heaven, please be good and Aunt Annie will take you over to your beds.'

Elizabeth had allowed the children to stay up but now she hoped that tiredness would eventually give way to sleep. Maybe they could face things better in the morning …

Compliant, the children went to bed, but could not sleep. They relived every moment of the hours before. Tomás Óg and Siobhán huddled together. They cried and cried, and there was no consoling them. When they did fall asleep, it was from exhaustion

A number of Volunteers arrived. They were stunned at the scene that greeted them, and realised that there were some practical issues to be dealt with. The body was dressed in full uniform and laid out again. Priests, Volunteers and family busied themselves to make the bedroom ready for the all night vigil. The disruption caused by the searchers was no longer detectable. The Volunteers set up a guard of honour and stood to attention at the bedside of their fallen leader.

Before any sympathisers arrived at the house the next morning, Elizabeth again gathered the children to say a prayer at the bedside of their father. The funeral was going to be a very public affair and it was best for the children to be prepared. 'There is no need to be afraid. Dada is gone to heaven and we are all going to say a special prayer.'

The room was silent. Their father lay still and pale in his green uniform. His hands lay by his sides. There were six men in the room, three at each side of the double bed. The family craved some private time with Tomás but the Volunteers stood to attention with sorrow deeply etched on their faces and Elizabeth could not ask them to leave. She understood that Tomás' men would not wish to leave their leader for even one second.

Elizabeth knew that it was very difficult for the children to grasp the situation. Siobhán had witnessed most of the horror of the night before and, aged eleven, was old enough to understand. She had crept in to say goodbye to her father. She was distraught and nobody knew yet how much of the murder the night before she had actually witnessed and what affect it would have on her over the next few days and throughout her life.

The dye was also cast for her baby brother – Tomás was almost five but seemed to her a baby. The words the killers had said would echo in his ears for life and years later he was destined to hear the same words – men would be coming for him and a gun would be put to his chest.

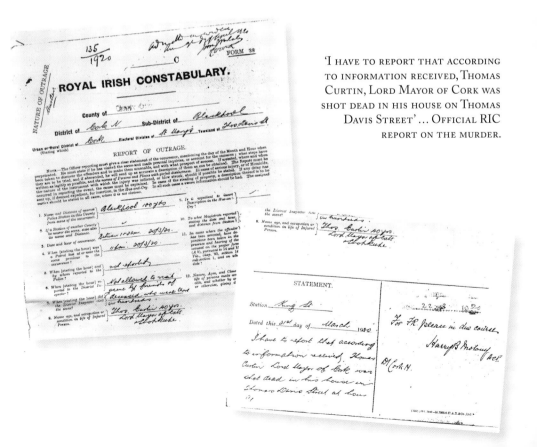

'I HAVE TO REPORT THAT ACCORDING TO INFORMATION RECEIVED, THOMAS CURTIN, LORD MAYOR OF CORK WAS SHOT DEAD IN HIS HOUSE ON THOMAS DAVIS STREET' … OFFICIAL RIC REPORT ON THE MURDER.

14

A City Stands Still and its Citizens Weep

Elizabeth had decisions to make. People surrounded her as the house filled up with press, photographers, undertakers, priests, city officials, Republicans, Sinn Féin members, neighbours, workers – the list was endless. Her children had to be foremost in her mind. Her elderly mother needed consoling and minding. Her energy was sapped and it was not even noon.

On the other hand, everyone was concerned for Elizabeth. She looked worn and drawn. Her pregnancy had not been trouble free and Elizabeth's family were doing their best to protect her from the endless questions and the decisions that needed to be made. The grave that Patrick, their baby son, had been buried in was not to be used. Terence MacSwiney and Fred Cronin arranged for a new plot to be purchased at the gates of St Finbarr's cemetery.

On Saturday night, the city was still. Elizabeth stood at the top of the stairs shrouded in mourning clothes, with her back to where the bullet mark was on the wall, and watched as the remains of her husband were carried down the narrow stairs. It was still less than twenty-four hours since the murder. The eerie sound of the pipers of his much-loved pipe band and the marching of his men surged through her head. The remains were removed from the house to the City Hall. A uniformed guard of honour surrounded the open coffin. A public outpouring of anguish, sorrow, disbelief and anger was displayed and the city was turned into a simmering cauldron of emotion.

Dignitaries, businessmen, politicians and sympathisers poured in from all over Ireland to pay their respects. Word had spread and many people felt a compulsion to travel to Cork to just be there. Throughout Saturday night and all day Sunday

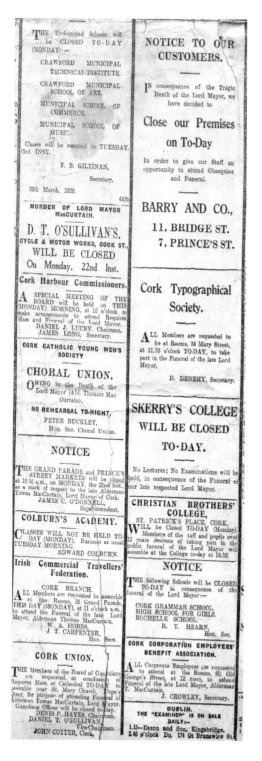

people of diverse interests and all walks of life queued for many hours to pay their respect to a man and his principles. For these principles he had paid the ultimate price – he had given his life. The citizens of Cork filed pass the corpse in horrified silence.

Many who had, until now, taken little interest in political affairs were so outraged that there was an outpouring of condemnation against the British establishment that was akin to the rage in Dublin at the execution of the 1916 leaders.

On Sunday night Tomás' body was moved – from lying in state at the City Hall – to the North Cathedral. Volunteers from all over Ireland lined the route. Men he had trained took the most active roles in the arrangements. The citizens of Cork crowded the pathways and there was not a policeman or a British soldier in sight. It was a time for silent respect and mourning. Official counters could not tally the correct number of people,

THE VOLUNTEER BODYGUARDS WHO CARRIED THE COFFIN; NOTICE OF FUNERAL ARRANGEMENTS AND OPPOSITE, NEWSPAPER NOTICES ANNOUNCING THE CLOSING OF MANY CORK PREMISES

but all agreed on a conservative figure of 10,000. Never before had Cork seen such crowds.

Elizabeth stood still as they began the ritual of closing the coffin. She turned at the last moment and noticed one of the Volunteers walking around stopping at regular intervals as he made his way inside the guard of honour on duty and around the edge of the coffin. Only later when she was handed a collection of buttons tied in a black ribbon did it register that he had been cutting the buttons off Tomás' uniform.

15

Silence

On Monday 22 March, the city of Cork came to a standstill. The shops closed. Every factory stood silent. Trams did not operate and the ships laden with their cargo sat low in the water. The docks were empty and the machinery lay idle. Nobody was told to stay away, but nobody turned up for work. Mourners poured into the city.

Uniformed Volunteers carried out their duties with the detail and precision that their commander had come to expect of them. It was the first time that the Volunteers had all appeared in public in the new uniform.

Elizabeth had an idea of what to expect at the funeral. All the arrangements had been talked through with her. She knew that Volunteers had come from all over Ireland and expected that there would therefore be a big gathering. But nothing prepared her for the sea of people that stretched out along the route in total silence. It took hours to pass them. The mass ended. Elizabeth watched Terry MacSwiney, Seán O'Hegarty, Joseph O'Connor

TWO BLACK HORSES DREW THE FIRST
CARRIAGE, WHICH WAS LADEN WITH FLOWERS.
THE TOP AND SIDES OF THE CARRIAGE WERE
ALMOST COMPLETELY COVERED WITH FLORAL
TRIBUTES, PREDOMINANTLY IN GREEN, WHITE
AND ORANGE THAT WERE HEAPED HIGH AND
TRAILING OVER THE SIDES

THE SECOND HORSE-DRAWN CARRIAGE CONTAINED THE COFFIN OF THE LORD MAYOR. HIS YOUNG SON TOMÁS ÓG CAN BE SEEN WALKING BEHIND

and Florence O'Donoghue shoulder the coffin to the hearse. The funeral procession left the cathedral at one o' clock.

It had been a heart-wrenching decision to allow Tomás Óg to walk behind the hearse. She had looked deeply into his eyes which since that Saturday morning had seen so much. Things nobody should have witnessed, certainly not a child, her child, now left without a father.

Jimmy would watch out for him and Terry Mac, his godfather, was never far away. The little boy looked so beautiful, a full head of curls framing an angelic face with piercing blue eyes. The little black suit with its wide bib and snow-white collar gave his slight frame a formal look. Siobhán, aged eleven years, and Síle, aged ten, were devastated. Dressed in mourning clothes they had sobbed their way through the church service. Máire was too young to under-

stand anything. Susie had held the three-year-old in her arms.

Two black horses drew the first carriage, which was laden with flowers. The top and sides of the carriage were almost completely covered with floral tributes that were heaped high and trailing over the sides. The carriage carrying the remains also had flowers piled high on the roof. There were two enormous wreaths beside the driver and his companion. The predominant colours were green, white and orange and the glass sides allowed the onlookers to view the flag-draped coffin.

The procession wound its way down Roman Street and John Redmond Street. At this point others were still joining the cortège. Carriages lined Shandon Street and organised societies and the general public, anxious to walk, waited along St Mary's Road. Marshals directed the crowds converging on the north side of the city. Cork's Volunteer pipe band, Volunteers, Cork Corporation, UCC dignitaries – the list of mourners seemed endless. The cortège

CIVIC BODIES AND SOCIETIES AND THE PUBLIC MADE UP THE END OF THE PROCESSION

then followed the route of King Street. Passing the doors of the RIC barracks from which the assassins had marched to carry out their treacherous deed, a foul murder, Elizabeth could not bear to look at the building. She stared straight ahead and concentrated on watching the carriages turn over the bridge and up Merchants Quay. There was hardly standing space for the crowds as it passed to continue its journey down Patrick Street, Grand Parade and out Washington Street to the Western Road and the new plot at the gates of St Finbarr's cemetery. Mourners who wanted to see the entire procession that morning had to stand for almost two hours. Women unashamedly wept openly.

The citizens of Cork had never witnessed a scene like this before. Many felt compelled not just to be there but also to walk. A number of men had brought their young sons to march with them. John Joseph O'Callaghan [Jack], only a child himself, led another group, proud to be walking with his sailor cap on his

THE EERIE SOUND OF THE PIPE BAND CARRIED ACROSS THE RIVERBANK

head, with his father Patrick behind keeping a watchful eye on his young son. The young Tomás walked behind the hearse with dignity, he seemed totally unaware that thousands of eyes were upon him Just looking at her little boy, dressed in his black pantaloon suit was such a poignant sight it brought fresh tears to Elizabeth's eyes. She found it hard to believe that she actually could still shed more tears. Jimmy was keeping a close eye on Tomás Óg but the child reassured him on a regular basis that he was fine. No he was not tired and he did not want to join Mama in the carriage. Seán and his other uncles walked behind him. Many familiar faces surrounded him.

The smell of flowers wafted all around them. Men, too many to count, carried various shaped wreaths in the procession. The whole ceremony seemed surreal. The clip clop of the horses hooves could be heard and their breath curled up like steam in the cold March air. Thousands upon thousands stood in silence. The eerie

SIOBHÁN AND SÍLE SAT STONY-FACED. MÁIRE WAS VERY WITHDRAWN
TOMÁS ÓG JUMPED OFF EILÍS' KNEE, HE WANTED TO SAY GOODBYE TO DADA

sound of the pipe band carried across the riverbank where the crowd also stood. People from all over the county and citizens of Cork in mourning took their place and walked to St Finbarr's cemetery on the outskirts of the town. Inside and outside the cemetery there was a sea of black. The choir sang, the priests chanted. Chairs were lined in two neat rows for the womenfolk to sit on.

Elizabeth, who was about five months pregnant, sat for the long ceremony. She had slept very little during the night but tried to rest, concerned about the well-being of her unborn child. She could not believe how still the children were. Siobhán and Síle sat stony-faced. Máire was very withdrawn. Mary's children were still in shock.

It was only at the end that Tomás Óg jumped off her knee, he wanted to say goodbye to Dada. How could he be expected to comprehend the concept of death? He went over to his Uncle Jimmy, stood motionless and watched as the coffin was lowered into the hole in the ground. Dada was gone.

HE WENT OVER TO HIS UNCLE JIMMY, STOOD MOTIONLESS AND WATCHED AS
THE COFFIN WAS LOWERED INTO THE HOLE IN THE GROUND.

The Last Post was sounded at the new plot near the gates. Shots were fired over the grave.

It was a heartbroken, sombre Terence MacSwiney who addressed the crowd:

> Although the great work, which has been done by the Lord Mayor of
> Cork has been interrupted by his murder, the Volunteer Movement
> will carry on as heretofore, another will take our dead leader's place.
> No matter how many lose their lives in the course of their duty, as
> did the Lord Mayor, another will always be found to take the lead.

It was not a time for a long oration. Nobody could adequately describe the character of the man being laid to rest. He was a truly great Irish man and a natural leader. A poet, musician and writer, the tributes went on. The day would come when not only Cork but also Ireland would know and acknowledge its loss.

Tomás Óg stood on the mound of fresh earth close to the gates of St Finbarr's cemetery. These events had made an indelible mark on the mind and character of this young boy. Unknown to him he was now a target. The elders in the family and the high-ranking Volunteers had already heard a rumour from informers within the RIC that the child would be a target if there were reprisals for the murder of the Lord Mayor. If tracking down the perpetrators of this crime and having justice was to be classed as reprisal, this was going to happen, as sure as day turned to night. It was just a question of when and where.

Jimmy, Elizabeth's brother, placed a hand on the shoulder of the young Tomás Mac Curtáin, looked around at his friends and nodded. He was in their charge from that day forth and for the foreseeable future, they would never be far from his side.

Hundreds lined up in front of the Lady Mayoress' seat to shake hands and sympathise with her. They had travelled from all over

THE LAST POST WAS SOUNDED AT THE NEW PLOT NEAR THE GATES. SHOTS WERE FIRED OVER THE GRAVE

Ireland and Elizabeth felt a strong sense of duty to meet as many of them as she could and to personally thank them for attending. The strain was getting too much for the mourning party and eventually the Volunteers on marshal duty redirected the stream of mourners around the far side of the grave to create a pathway that would enable Elizabeth and the children to be escorted to the waiting carriages.

It was over for today at least. Elizabeth gathered her children close to her and returned home to Thomas Davis Street, exhausted. She was still coming to terms with what had happened in place of the surprise birthday celebrations they had planned for her beloved husband. The walls on the landing had been washed clean but the hole remained in the plaster where the bullet had lodged. What was the future to bring her and her family in the days and years that lay ahead? Only God knew and in Him she had to place her trust.

16

The Aftermath

Oh God, how she hated the house, hated the area, hated the factory. Everybody was doing their best but how could they even begin to comprehend this living nightmare?

Daytime brought no release. Dawn only confirmed that the nightmares were true – Elizabeth was exhausted both mentally and physically. There were still so many demands upon her time. She was surrounded by people but she felt so alone. She was still trying to operate the house with some semblance of normality for the children's sake. Her sisters – Annie and Susie – were caring for Mama and Jimmy was keeping a watchful eye on Tomás. His welfare was utmost in her thoughts, as he seemed to be the one most at risk.

She knew it was going to be just a matter of time before those responsible for her husband's death were tracked down. Michael Collins had assured her that he would personally see that there

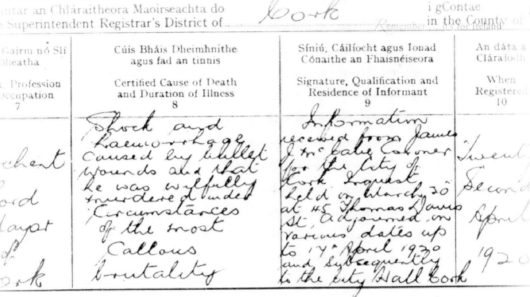

CERTIFIED CAUSE OF DEATH: SHOCK AND HAEMORRHAGE CAUSED BY BULLET WOUNDS AND THAT HE
WAS WILFULLY MURDERED UNDER CIRCUMSTANCES OF THE MOST CALLOUS BRUTALITY

would not be a stone left unturned in tracking down the murderers of his friend. She was never to know the exact details but Elizabeth did learn that when the time came Tomás' own Cork No. 1 brigade avenged their commander's murder using his own weapon – the very gun that had lain under their crying baby on the night he was murdered.

Elizabeth heard a rumour that the British army had come to Cork in March to arrest her husband. They wished to interview him in connection with a plan that had been uncovered to kill Lord French. Inspector Swanzy had sent them back to Dublin to check their facts and he said that Tomás Mac Curtáin, Lord Mayor of Cork was no threat to the British security forces.

THE JURY TOOK LESS THAN TWO HOURS TO RETURN A VERDICT OF WILFUL MURDER

Had the murder been planned weeks before it was carried out? The true facts would never be known.

The Verdict of the Inquest

There really could only be one verdict – murder.

Just after noon on 17 April 1920 the jury, having heard all the evidence, were sent from the court by Coroner McCabe. They were to deliberate and report back. It took them less than two hours to agree and write out a full report:

> We find that the late Alderman Tomás Mac Curtáin, Lord Mayor of Cork, died from shock and haemorrhage caused by bullet wounds and that he was wilfully murdered under the circumstances of

Mr Coroner:- As we are now nearing the end of the local evidence that is to be produced, and as it has appeared in the Public Press, without official contradiction, that the Authorities in Dublin Castle have information as to who the murderers of the late Lord Mayor are and as to the motives, which inspired the murder: in order to enable the jury to arrive at a just conclusion touching the circumstances into which we are enquiring, we are of opinion that His Excellency Lord French and Sir John Taylor, Under Secretary, should be summoned by you, Sir, as witnesses in this enquiry,

On behalf of the Jury.

William J. Barry.

(Foreman).

12 - 4 - 1920.

the most callous brutality and that the murder was organised and carried out by the Royal Irish Constabulary, officially directed by the British Government and we return a verdict of wilful murder against David Lloyd George, Prime Minister of England, Lord French, Lord Lieutenant of Ireland, Ian MacPherson, late Chief Secretary of Ireland, Acting Inspector General Smith of the Royal Irish Constabulary, Divisional Inspector Clayton of the Royal Irish Constabulary, District Inspector Swanzy and some unknown members of the Royal Irish Constabulary.

We most strongly condemn the system at present in vogue of carrying out raids at unreasonable hours.

We tender to Mrs Mac Curtain and family our sincerest sympathy in their terrible bereavement; this sympathy we extend to the citizens of Cork in the loss they have sustained by the death of one so eminently capable of directing their civic administration.

On various occasions, whilst reading the report aloud, the coroner was interrupted by applause. Everybody had felt that there could only be one verdict but to have the actual name of the British prime minister called out in court and found guilty was more than the majority of the crowd thought would happen.

On 21 April, a messenger arrived from the City Hall about 9.30 a.m. with a private letter for Elizabeth from Terence MacSwiney.

She sat down with a heavy heart to read it:

My dear Lizzie,

You see I'm not standing on ceremony with the death of Tomás R.I.P. My own responsibilities as Tomás Óg's godfather are in my mind and for that reason there should be no formality between us. I meant to write to you at once after the funeral to impress on you

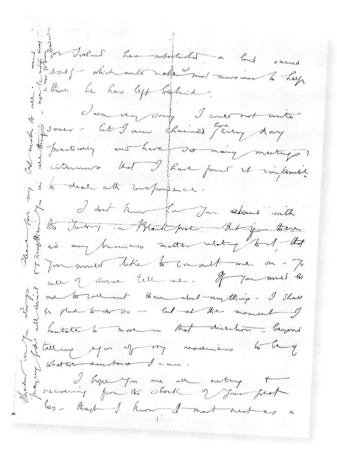

TERENCE WROTE
TO ELIZABETH: MY
LONG AND INTIMATE
ASSOCIATION WITH
TOMÁS THROUGH GOOD
FORTUNE AND ADVERSITY
IN OUR COMMON WORK
FOR IRELAND HAS
ESTABLISHED A BOND
SACRED ITSELF WHICH
WOULD MAKE ME MOST
ANXIOUS TO HELP THOSE
HE HAS LEFT BEHIND

that any service I can ever be to you or the children I shall only be too happy to perform and shall look upon it even as a duty. You must never hesitate to ask me to do anything that is in my power to do. Even if the obligations referred to do not rest on me, my long and intimate association with Tomás through good fortune and adversity in our common work for Ireland has established a bond sacred itself which would make me most anxious to help those he has left behind.

I am very sorry I could not write sooner – but I am chained here every day practically and have so many meetings and interviews I don't know how you stand with the factory in Blackpool. But if there is any business matter relating to it that you would like to consult me on – you will of course tell me. If you would like me to call out there about anything – I shall be glad to do so but at the moment I hesitate to move in that direction beyond telling you of my readiness to bring whatever assistance I can. I hope you are all resting and recovering from the shock of your great loss 'though I know it must rest as a shadow on you always. Please give my best wishes to all and praying that God will direct and strengthen you in all things.

Mise le meas
Terry

Elizabeth reflected. The two men had held such dreams and hopes and had fostered a love of their city. Tomás was now gone and it was up to Terry to keep the dream alive. Tomás had made such a wise choice asking Terry to be Tomás Óg's godfather. Her concern now was to make sure that she would not be the cause of making extra demands on his time. Much as she appreciated his offer of help, how could she ask him to spare some of his precious time when deep in her heart she felt that he himself had so little time left. Her premonition of his early demise was to come true.

Terence MacSwiney and the corporation started a Memorial Fund for the Lord Mayor's family. Donations big and small were coming into the office at the City Hall. It was the only practical way that many people could help. Terence himself had given most of his personal savings to the fund.

Terence MacSwiney replied to one of the contributors, Lady Fitzgerald Arnott:

24th April, 1920

Madam,

I beg to acknowledge with thanks your letter of the 13th inst. enclosing subscription £10.00 to the Mac Curtáin Memorial Fund. The official receipt has been sent. I had to defer answering your questions as to the murder until the inquest was concluded, as I could not properly pass judgement on the matter when it was *sub judice*.

Lord French and the English Press violated all precedent and decency in circulating their slanders while the inquiry was proceeding. If they had any material evidence to put forward, the place to do so was before the court. We on our side would not permit any rejoinder to the slander because the matter was *sub judice*. And we were most anxious nothing should be said that would in any way impair the strictest and most impartial inquiry.

As you repeated your question in a letter to my secretary I assume that you have not read the detailed evidence as published in the *Cork Press*. This evidence is overwhelming and the verdict of the jury is the only possible verdict for those seeking the truth. I can not in the limitations of a letter enumerate all the points, but will mention some of those outstanding.

Two things stand out clearly (1) that the murder was carried out by the police; (2) that it was organised officially – the latter making the Government responsible.

1: Evidence against the police; The men who formed the

> Lord French and the English Press violated all precedent and decency in circulating their slanders while the inquiry was proceeding.

murder party were seen by independent witnesses marching like trained men in King Street, on St Patrick's Hill and in Blackpool area. Policemen in uniform were seen with them on St Patrick's Hill by Nurse Daunt from the window of the private hospital in which she was engaged. Two policemen in uniform held up Witness McCarthy in Blackpool close to the late Lord Mayor's house and compelled him to make a detour to avoid the house when the murder was about to take place. The murder party was seen marching through King Street before the murder and they passed two police patrols. The police did not accost them or report to King Street police barracks. Here is the evidence of Lamplighter Desmond, as quoted by the Counsel, whilst standing there at twenty minutes to two o'clock, he saw a body of men in single file and advancing in quick march and carrying rifles, enter King Street barracks. He saw them go up the steps. They were admitted after a light knock and he describes the door being unlocked and the chain taken off, as no one could, except he actually witnessed the operation.

2: There is much weighty evidence against the police besides the foregoing. The significance of it all is best seen in the Crown Solicitor's statement. I quote his exact words as reported. This was a murder in which there were engaged between forty and fifty men. They would remember the Lady Mayoress gave evidence of one group of men numbering from ten to fifteen – disguised men. Some 500 yards away, two men gave evidence of a group of from twenty-two to twenty-four men, and they had evidence of a third group in York Street. Taking these three groups together, they would find there must have been between forty and fifty men engaged in the murder. He always liked to look at a charge and speak plainly. If the suggestion was to be made and if they were dealing with forty or fifty policemen, then this was a charge of murder against every policeman in the City of Cork. It would be humanly impossible to have forty policemen out that night without the consent and connivance of every policeman in Cork.

The fact was brought irresistibly home to the mind of every one present. In connection with this, you should study the evidence touching D. I. Swanzy himself, the responsible police officer in the area in which the murder was committed.

You refer to the slanderous story that the Lord Mayor was murdered by Sinn Féiners and you say you had it definitely from a certain gentleman. You suggested calling this gentleman before the Courts. The proper people to call were called. Lord French and Sir John Taylor. They refused to come. Were they in a position to verify the story, they could destroy the Republican movement in this generation. The conclusion is obvious. The lie has come home to them and helped to lay the guilt at their own door.

The pain did not ease and as the day began to dawn Elizabeth was writhing in agony.

On 8 July, Elizabeth woke with a searing pain in her stomach. Her body had taken some mistreatment over the last few weeks. The doctor had warned her that she would have to get plenty of rest. This pregnancy had not been easy from the start and she had struggled on a daily basis, so she now had no choice but to slow down. She had never really regained her strength since the night of the murder. Everything that she had done as a matter of routine before now seemed to be a huge effort. It was not just her pregnant figure that made things difficult but

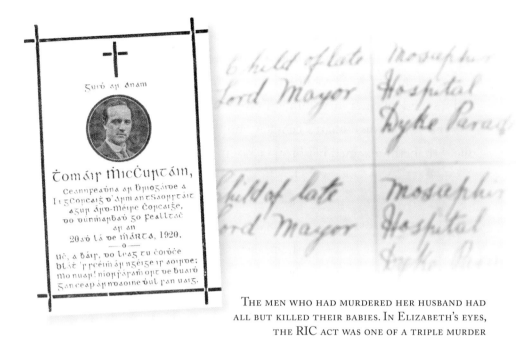

THE MEN WHO HAD MURDERED HER HUSBAND HAD
ALL BUT KILLED THEIR BABIES. IN ELIZABETH'S EYES,
THE RIC ACT WAS ONE OF A TRIPLE MURDER

also that she really had no enthusiasm for anything that needed to be done. She repeated errands and house duties out of habit rather than with the slightest thought.

The pain did not ease and as the morning came Elizabeth was writhing in agony. She had been reluctant to call her sisters in the middle of the night but she could wait no longer. She needed them to call the doctor.

The doctor arrived and Elizabeth was immediately transferred to the hospital on Dyke Parade. At approximately noon, Elizabeth gave birth. The two beautiful baby girls were stillborn. Elizabeth, no stranger now to the pain of loss, was consumed once again with grief and cried for her beautiful babies.

Jimmy and Hannah went to St Finbarr's cemetery that very same day to bury the babies. Elizabeth lay in a hospital bed as part of her was buried once again in the family plot. Baby Patrick was to be joined by his two little sisters. Room would be made in heaven for two more angels. Elizabeth cried, her heart was broken. How much more could she withstand? The words sorrow and loss had taken on new dimensions.

The visit to St Finbarr's cemetery on 8 July was a poignant one. Elizabeth imagined her brother Jimmy and her sisters carrying the tiny white coffins. In her mind, she took every step with them. Past the green mound of earth just inside the gates. The grave of her husband commanded the area. She had asked them to stop and say a prayer. The family grave was up the long main path of the cemetery and almost at the very end on the left hand side, a few rows in. Her heart was truly broken, as she mentally made the journey with them.

For the past few months, the impending birth of the baby had kept her going. She had not known they were twins. She knew that she had to keep herself well for the sake of the baby, so she watched what she ate and took plenty of rest. The doctors could give her no reason for what had happened. They had been two perfectly formed baby girls – their deaths were inexplicable.

Life, as ever went on outside her house. Terence MacSwiney was elected Lord Mayor and the roller coaster of events seemed never ending. Letters of sympathy from all over the world were still pouring in to the City Hall. Urban councils, organisations, committees in cities, towns and villages all over Ireland, England and America expressed their outrage at the murder of her husband and their sympathy for Elizabeth and her children.

A few months later Elizabeth was shocked to be told of the arrest of Terry Mac on 12 August and his being sent to England. Shortly after he began his final protest against the tyranny meted out to his beloved Ireland. She had only heard the day before that a number of Republican prisoners had gone on hunger strike in

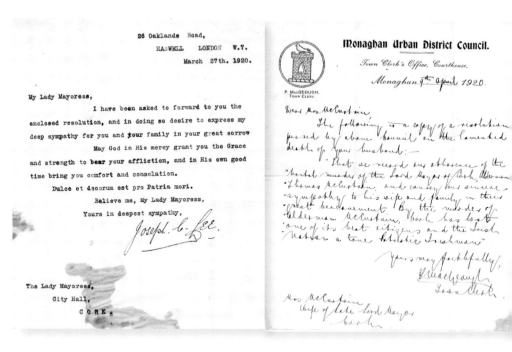

26 Oaklands Road,
HANWELL LONDON W.7.
March 27th. 1920.

My Lady Mayoress;

I have been asked to forward to you the enclosed resolution, and in doing so desire to express my deep sympathy for you and your family in your great sorrow

May God in His mercy grant you the Grace and strength to bear your affliction, and in His own good time bring you comfort and consolation.

Dulce et decorum est pro Patria mori.

Believe me, My Lady Mayoress,

Yours in deepest sympathy,

Joseph. C. Lee.

The Lady Mayoress,
City Hall,
C O R K.

Monaghan Urban District Council.

Town Clerk's Office, Courthouse,

Monaghan 9th April 1920.

P. MacGEOUGH.
TOWN CLERK.

Dear Mrs McCurtain

The following is a copy of a resolution passed by above Council on the lamented death of your husband:—

"That we record our abhorrence of the brutal murder of the Lord Mayor of Cork, Alderman Thomas McCurtain, and convey our sincere sympathy to his wife and family in their great bereavement. By the murder of Alderman McCurtain, Cork has lost one of its best citizens and the Irish Nation a true patriotic Irishman"

Yours very faithfully,
P. MacGeough,
Town Clerk.

Mrs McCurtain
Wife of late Lord Mayor
Cork

LETTERS OF SYMPATHY FROM ALL OVER THE WORLD POURED IN TO THE CITY HALL

Cork Gaol. Not a day went by but something was happening. The city was reaching boiling point. The week earlier curfew patrols had been fired on almost every night. The news that RIC District Inspector Swanzy had been shot in Lisburn came on 22 August. That news brought her no comfort, but justice, in part, had been served.

King George V asked Lloyd George to find a way to end the hunger strike of Terry Mac. Lloyd George remained inflexible and no move was made by the British government to find a solution. If the options were to be death or release, it would be death. His long hunger strike was bravely endured and Elizabeth kept in constant contact with his sister Annie. The agonising days and weeks led to months until his ravaged body, having fought to the end, gave up after seventy-four days of hunger strike.

Volunteer Joe Murphy, who was also on hunger strike at Cork Gaol, died the same day. Elizabeth felt for his family and sent her sincere condolences. She knew that his comrades in H Coy, 2nd Batt 1st Cork brigade would never forget his contribution. His suffering, that had gone on for seventy-six days, received very little coverage as the world media focused their attention on the struggle of Terence MacSwiney.

The death of an Irish Lord Mayor in an English jail brought the eyes of the world to focus on Ireland and her fight for freedom again.

The Volunteers accompanied his body as it was shipped back to Ireland. Again, thousands gathered as the coffin arrived at the quayside.

It was like a *deja vu* when Elizabeth attended the funeral of Terry. The same sorrow-etched faces of the Volunteers haunted her. Men who had served and loved two commanders had seen both lives extinguished in their prime. Once again the city was engulfed in sorrow.

'Yes, tell them nothing matters if they don't give in – nothing – nothing – the last moment – that's the important time … what's the use of being alive if you give in.'

Terry's own words came to Elizabeth's mind. In 1914 he had written a play, *The Revolutionist*, and in it the hero said, 'Yes, tell them nothing matters if they don't give in – nothing – nothing – the last moment – that's the important time … what's the use of being alive if you give in.'

Elizabeth's heart went out to her friends, the MacSwiney sisters, as she knew what they were suffering. When Elizabeth's carriage pulled up with the funeral cortège at the gates of the cemetery the perfume from the flowers made her nauseous. The chanting of the priests, the crowds, the past and the present funeral all mingled in her mind. The plot of land just inside the gates of St Finbarr's cemetery was to be used once again and Terry was laid on the right of his best friend – her husband. It was fitting, as in many cases he was Tomás' right hand man. The two of them had gone so fast. This year was turning into a river of tears and continuous sorrow.

Fr Dominic was broken-hearted. He had held these two men in such high esteem and had done everything he could for them. Along with Fr Albert they continued to show their admiration for the fallen leaders by standing by, and advising, the men of the Cork brigade. He was not to know that he and Fr Albert would be sent into exile for the dedication they gave to the cause of Irish freedom.

Elizabeth had not yet replied to or received all the letters of condolence that continued to pour in. Now, these same people and committees were sending their condolences to Muriel, Terry's wife, his baby daughter, Máire and to his brothers and sisters.

Fr Dominic was broken-hearted

A bond developed between the MacSwiney sisters and the Mac Curtain family that endured for years. The Mac Curtain girls had gone to school at Scoil Ita which was founded by the MacSwineys. The sisters had tried to persuade Tomás not to send fees for them, but Tomás had insisted. How could the school be expected to survive if the parents were to take advantage of the generosity of the sisters? Times were tough for everybody.

Her son Tomás had lost a father and a godfather who were to be remembered as two of the most influential soldiers and politicians that Cork had ever reared. Sadly, neither man had the opportunity to show his full potential.

A sense of loneliness and emptiness engulfed Elizabeth. She was weary in mind and body and felt the years of hardship had caught up with her. She had many times reassured Tomás that she was all right and that she knew exactly what she was taking on when she married him. They had wanted a large family and their own business, but she understood that his first duty was always going to be to the struggle for Irish freedom. Her contribution was to keep the home fires burning and she made sure that there was always a warm loving home for the family. Now what did she have? His death to mourn, and the death of her beautiful baby girls. The men who had murdered her husband had all but killed their babies. In Elizabeth's eyes, the RIC act was one of a triple murder.

Two of the most influential soldiers and politicians that Cork had ever reared. Sadly, neither man had the opportunity to show his full potential.

The fund had collected a considerable amount of money and everybody thought it was in Elizabeth's best interest to move from Thomas Davis Street. As long as she continued to live in the house where the horrific murder had taken place, she would not be able to mend totally in mind or body. She needed rest and plenty of it.

A suitable house was found for the family at 1 Grosvenor Place, on the north side of Cork, high above the river Lee. The headache of running the mill was now over and Elizabeth was able to turn her attention totally to getting better and rearing the children.

Around the country it soon became clear that the RIC could not keep control. The Black and Tans had not achieved their aim of returning law and order and on 20 October, the first battalion of the Auxiliary police arrived in Cork.

Jimmy was still involved with the Volunteers and Elizabeth was glad to have the distraction of the lads coming and going. Her kitchen remained a hive of activity and she followed events with great interest, often pausing to reflect on how proud Tomás would have been of the continuing fight.

The Auxies ran riot around the countryside and the British government could not wipe its hands of these actions. It was their force carrying out the atrocities and therefore the ultimate responsibility lay with them. The Auxies wreaked havoc throughout the country and were very unruly, but guerrilla warfare was working for the Volunteers.

The Mac Curtain home commanded a panoramic view over the city of Cork. It was searched and ransacked many times. Elizabeth had put a copy of the 1916 Proclamation up on the wall and a plate from the Lord Mayor's dinner service that she had been given. They smashed her plate to the floor. She considered herself

> The Auxies wreaked havoc throughout the country and were very unruly, but guerrilla warfare was working for the Volunteers.

very fortunate to be able to send it to Dublin to have the china stitched. When Elizabeth's house was ransacked and many valuable items went missing, there was nothing she could do. At the start, it was only the Black and Tans but now the Auxiliaries were also causing chaos in Cork City and county.

Shooting at farmers in the countryside became a pastime. It was considered great fun by the Auxies to discharge their guns at the ground near their feet to see how high the farmers would jump or how fast they could run. Many were maimed or killed by this cruel pastime. Houses were ransacked. Urban and rural residents were united in their hatred of the Auxies and the Black and Tans. The regular army stayed in the background. A hatred of the British regime was not just an undercurrent anymore – it was rampant. Elizabeth was always anxious to get news of any Volunteer action. She prayed daily that all out at Ballyknockane, Tomás' old home, would remain safe.

When General Tom Barry, who was serving abroad with the British army, heard of the struggle that was going on, he quit the empire force to return to Cork. He became the leader of the Flying Column, Cork No. 3 brigade. If he was to fight for the freedom of small nations, none was to be higher on his list than his own. He set up a flying column and guerrilla warfare came to the fore. Although the Volunteers may not be able to defeat the British forces, if they hit them by surprise and quickly faded back into the countryside, the British would be unable to conquer them. Surprise, attack the enemies' weakest, most vulnerable area and disperse were the orders. This could only be done with the help of the locals – the ordinary (or extraordinary) people lending their support. Tom Barry's men were at war. The atrocities committed by the crown forces were met face-on by the Volunteers.

Local farmers helped the Volunteers to retreat thus putting their homes and farms at risk. Local residents paid a high price. Public opinion had taken a u-turn. The start of the century had shown the Irish nation to be subservient to the demands of England and now freedom and independence were the battle cry of the day. Small RIC barracks around the county continued to be raided – arms were acquired and the staff of these barracks retreated to the city. When Elizabeth read of the attacks in the newspaper, it always brought a smile to her face as she remembered Tomás' excitement when his men had taken the first action back in January 1919. That now seemed such a long time ago.

The atrocities committed by the crown forces were met face-on by the Volunteers.

All that the Auxies, Black and Tans and the British army could do was to try to contain the freedom fighters. They looted and burned many villages and were hated rather than accepted by the community. The Black and Tans failed miserably and then the Auxies were let loose to do their worst. They totalled approximately 1,500 men and were commanded by General F. P. Crozier. When they arrived in Ireland, they were first sent to the Curragh for training and then despatched to various corners of Ireland. Most of these men had seen action during the First World War and they fought hard and dirty. They drank to excess and the citizens of Cork endured their antics.

A hatred of the very sight of these foul-mouthed, hard drinkers and cantankerous troublemakers was festering throughout local communities. The Volunteers could and would take action. The more the Auxies picked on defenceless women, children and widows the more it spurred on the action of the Volunteers.

Tom Barry's flying column was a unit of well-trained, well-disciplined men. He planned an attack on the Auxies and organised an ambush in which seventeen Auxies were killed. Barry lost three of his men but showed the county that the Auxies were not invincible.

Seán O'Hegarty was now the commanding officer of Tomás' No. 1 brigade and he wanted the city to build on the success of the county's fight. From a look-out house across from Victoria barracks it was established that a nightly patrol of Auxies left the barracks after tea and two units went in a convoy down the Old Youghal Road and turned off at Dillon's Cross for the city centre. James O'Mahony from the first battalion made an in-depth study of the area.

On 9 December, Seán O'Donoghue with Bob Langford second in command, rounded up their unit for action. The twelve men were ready. They had decided to strike the Auxies as near to Victoria Barracks as possible and so the end of Balmoral Terrace at the corner of Dillon's Cross was picked as the ideal location. Everybody knew O'Callaghan's field lay over the wall. A long run down brought you into the Glen area and relative safety.

> Barry lost three of his men but showed the county that the Auxies were not invincible.

They had researched the planned action but the patrol didn't come out at the expected time so the ambush had to be cancelled. It was a night of anticipation and tension that ended in no action at all. Members of Cumann na mBan collected the grenades and Annie Barry stored these in her house on Ballyhooley Road. Since Tomás' death, the Volunteers refused to use Elizabeth's house for either storing arms or as a safe house. She offered the use of her home on a regular basis, but everything possible was done to protect their leader's widow and children. Her sympathy for the cause meant that the house was under constant surveillance. It had been too risky to involve her in any action.

Cumann na mBan had a huge network of support in place to help the Volunteers and it was particularly strong in Cork. The men were anxious not to involve the women folk in particularly dangerous situations but at times like this, they had little choice. The Volunteers took home their own firearms as everybody had to be home before curfew at 10.00 p.m. They would live to fight another day.

> Cumann na mBan had a huge network of support in place to help the Volunteers and it was particularly strong in Cork.

On 11 December, word came that there would most definitely be a patrol – not only that but Captain James Kelly was to be with the trucks. He was a notorious member of the British intelligence force. It was teatime when Seán O'Donoghue got word to round up his unit. With such short notice, he could only muster up four others for action – Seán Healy, Michael Baylor, James O'Mahony, Gussie O'Leary. The ever-reliable Annie Barry brought back the grenades. Her importance should not be under-estimated. Without a safe house in the area and the dedication of Cumann na mBan members many an action would have been doomed to failure before it started. Michael Kenny was to act as the scout. He had worked inside Victoria barracks as a tradesman, knew many of the soldiers by sight and had seen Kelly on numerous occasions. He was the best equipped of the Volunteers to halt the trucks and give the nod as to which one contained Kelly. Just after 8.00 p.m., two lorries left Victoria barracks with about twelve men in each. They took the expected route down the Youghal Road. Kenny managed to get the patrol to slow down and Michael Baylor and Gussie O'Leary concentrated all their efforts on the first truck with O'Donoghue, Healy and O'Mahony opening fire on the second lorry.

Utter confusion ensued. The units in the barracks heard the exchange of fire and quickly dispatched reinforcements. Men, bloodhounds and lights descended on the area. The place was lit up like a Christmas tree. The five quickly reacted. They dispersed down their various planned escapes routes. Three scattered in the direction of the city, leaving O'Donoghue and O'Mahony to head off in the direction of Dublin Hill.

The last two moved swiftly and when they arrived at Delany's farm they hid some of the arms and went their separate ways.

The raid was considered a success. They did not get Kelly but the rest of the action went off as planned. Jimmy could hardly contain himself when telling the story to Elizabeth – it was like he was there himself such was his attention to detail and his storytelling. He was not allowed to relate anything in front of the children. Siobhán's love of drama and her imagination had not abated over the years. Elizabeth could still recall the shock and horror of Mairín Casey's father when he was repeating the story of the anti-Christ that Siobhán had told his daughter. Privately Elizabeth was convinced that when her back was turned Jimmy

> Men, bloodhounds and lights descended on the area. The place was lit up like a Christmas tree.

No risk would be taken and nothing would be allowed happen to the 'Mac Curtáin boy'.

was most definitely telling the children the stories and of course, the Volunteers were on a pedestal for them.

Tomás Óg already knew that his forefather Liam Curtin had fought at the battle of the Boyne, at Aughrim and at Limerick and that he was killed at Dromboy in 1724. The tales from then to now were never far from Jimmy's lips. Where would she be without Jimmy? If he was not with Tomás Óg at any given moment, one of his friends was. They never had the child out of their sight. That was the way it was since the night Tomás was murdered and that was the way it would stay. No risk would be taken and nothing would be allowed happen to the 'Mac Curtáin boy'.

Tomás Óg

17

Repercussions

The commanders of the Auxies, within Victoria barracks, were furious. They almost ignited with rage – the embarrassment of such an audacious raid at their very doorstep. A swift and hard punishment would have to be inflicted to regain the upper hand in the city. Later that night, patrols poured out of the barracks, descended on the houses at Dillon's Cross and burned a number of them to the ground. The Auxies were out for revenge and were given a free hand.

Elizabeth and her neighbours were out at their doors watching the flames rising. There was no way of finding out, at this time, whose house was on fire.

At about 10.00 p.m., a fire was noticed in Grants of Patrick Street. By now, there were dozens of Auxies parading down the street. News of various fires poured into the office of the chief fire officer, Captain Hutson. Soon the fire in Grants was out of control, the flames from the Munster Arcade were now spreading into

Egans and down the line – Roches Stores, Cashs, the Lee Cinema, and the whole block was soon engulfed.

Jimmy, came up York Hill to tell her that it was even worse than they had first thought. He listed out all the shops that were burning out of control. There was no hope that the fire engines could contain the blaze that raged back from Patrick Street to Cook Street and Marlboro Street. Virtually every place seemed alight.

Elizabeth implored him to stay in and be safe. Curfew time had come and anybody out would be shot, with no questions asked. He had already put himself at risk by going up to Dillon's Cross and walking into town.

Elizabeth knew that he would not rest easy until he had word of the lads but now she was putting her foot down. He was not going out again. Everybody was terrified – men, women, priests, nobody was spared. The army controlled the city and they allowed the Auxies to destroy at will. Beatings, shootings, burning and looting kept them occupied as the night wore on. As they drank, the crimes became more brutal and more out of control. It seemed that the whole city was going to go up in flames.

As the city burned, divisions of the Auxies up in the north side visited well-known Republican households. The trail of the men escaping from the ambush might have led them to Delany's – making them targets. They went to the family home of Jeremiah and

> There was no hope that the fire engines could contain the blaze that raged … virtually every place seemed alight.

Cornelius Delany of F Company of the Cork No. 1 brigade. They were taken from their beds and shot in front of their families.

Looting started. As dawn neared, the City Hall and the Carnegie Free Library were set alight. The clock on top of City Hall chimed out as if crying for attention. It could not be saved and fell silent.

None of the adults at 1 Grosvenor Place slept that night. There was no way of knowing where this was going to stop. Endless pots of tea were made and stories retold and of course Jimmy went right back to recalling the tales of the Fenians – he was incorrigible.

Elizabeth heard that the ambush was the reason for the burning of the city. It appeared more logical that the ambush was just an excuse to move into action. Various snippets of conversations had been overheard as to which shop to burn, etc.

The Tans and Auxies had marched in formation systematically setting fire to pre-arranged sites. She felt it was not a random action. She talked it over with Hannah and Jimmy, but they could not reach agreement on what had started this night of terror.

Mrs Barry had her shop at 77 Patrick's Street. She heard a rumour that the 'Tans' were going to burn her side of the street the following night. It was a question of all hands on deck to remove as much stock as they could from the shop. The English's, fellow traders from the market, had a cart and lent it to her to move as much as possible to her home opposite the Poor Clare's Convent, on College Road. The wheel came off the first cart and for years the story went down in the Barry household that they had caused the first traffic jam in Cork – passers-by got a glimpse of the mannequins piled up on the back of the cart, heading off in the direction of University College, Cork.

The official report filed by Major F. R. Eastwood of the seven-

THE BURNT EMBERS OF THE CITY SPREAD OUT IN FRONT OF HER AND THERE REMAINED
A SMELL OF BURNING IN THE AIR

teenth infantry read that between 11.00 p.m. on Saturday 11
December and 5.30 a.m. on Sunday 12 December 1920 the city
was in the complete control of the military. Only three arrests had
been made in a city that had been burned, looted and terrorised.

18

Another Christmas and a New Year

T he next day Elizabeth stood outside her home. It was bitterly cold and she drew her shawl tightly across her shoulders. Despite all that had recently happened there was laughter coming from the house. Children were resilient and there was an air of anticipation as they waited for Christmas Day.

She could not escape from her own thoughts. She was still dressed in mourning colours and was broken-hearted. The burnt embers of the city spread out in front of her and a smell of burning remained in the air. A cloud of smoke shrouded the city like a veil of sorrow and despair. Surely, the year 1920 in Cork would go down in the annals of history.

The city had lost its first Republican Lord Mayor. The civilians had struggled with coming to terms with his murder. It was closely followed by the hunger strike and the subsequent death of Terence MacSwiney and other republican prisoners.

Many indiscriminate murders had taken place. Now in the latest atrocity, the Auxies had done their best to burn Cork to the ground.

How did the British government think the people of Cork would react?

It should have known what to expect. Elizabeth knew that Rebel Cork might be down in spirit just now as it had been a dreadful year but there would be an outcry and Cork would rebuild itself – and not just with bricks and mortar. Cork people were fighters. They had been for generations and now would be no different. The lost lives would not be in vain. Cork Volunteers would regroup, in the name of their fallen leaders, and focus on the fight that was yet to be won – the fight for Irish freedom.

Life had changed irrevocably. Had all this happened in just one year? How could that be? Her life was in tatters and her health was deteriorating. She knew the searing pains she was suffering were not normal and she had been told the day before that the doctors were deeply concerned about the state of her lungs. Her next visit was scheduled for the New Year. She would then be told her initial test results.

Her beautiful city lay like a burnt out carcass in front of her. Black misshapen columns stood in the place of familiar shops in Patrick Street. The columns looked like giant grotesque figures on the skyline in the dusk. There was nothing left. Would this abyss of destruction and the all-engulfing personal sorrow drag her down? This could not be the end; this would not be the end – she had to think of the children.

Elizabeth went back indoors and climbed up the stairs. She stood at her bedroom window. It was not just the cold that chilled her right to the bones, but also the feeling of trepidation about what lay ahead.

BLACK MISSHAPEN COLUMNS STOOD IN THE PLACE OF FAMILIAR SHOPS

Her gaze fixed on her dressing-table. Hanging on her mirror were the buttons from Tomás' uniform. Next to her bottle of cologne, in its original box lay his Tara brooch and his Fáinne. Symbols of the loves of his life and the principles he held so dear. She would give the brooch to Tomás Óg and he would wear it when he led out the Volunteer Pipe band. The Fáinne would have to be earned by him in the years ahead. Her eyes rested on the little book next to his rosary beads. She held the book that Tomás loved so much close to her. He had turned to the book for comfort in his time of need. Quotes from *The Imitation of Christ* had given Tomás comfort and direction. It was well worn and the cover showed its constant usage.

Her husband was dead and her city lay in cinders. Her time of need was now.

She still had the letter Tomás had sent her in 1917. Through a veil of tears, she struggled to focus her eyes to reread it:

> May God grant it, but if in his wisdom the goal is not yet near,
> then thank God that this generation has upheld the honour of our
> century and can hand on to the next the cause and fight unsullied
> by dishonour and shame.
>
> > Our own we want, our own we'll have …

Tears poured down her face. It would take all of her strength to live her life true and committed to the cause of Irish freedom. The cross she was given to carry for the rest of her days seemed to be too heavy for any human to bear. The price of freedom was high. She would survive this pain because of her faith and her belief that her country was worth the sacrifices that she had been called upon to make. The pain was almost unbearable. She felt Tomás' presence beside her and heard him lovingly whisper to her the very words she had said to him as he lay dying in her arms:

'Remember darling, it's all for Ireland.'

A Family Grieves

19

The Family left Behind

Elizabeth was diagnosed with tuberculosis and was overcome with worry – what would become of her family? The outlook was very bleak and her heart ached. Whatever was to become of her and more to the point what was to become of her five children who had already suffered so much pain, disruption and loss? The years Tomás had spent in jail and exile had meant that her babies had spent many months fatherless. His murder had been committed in front of their eyes.

The doctor told her that there was virtually no hope of survival unless she was prepared to try a radical new treatment provided only in Switzerland. A pheumo-thorax procedure was her only chance and that had no guarantees. It was decided that Elizabeth would go to Switzerland and that Siobhán, as the eldest, would go with her. The rest of the children would stay with Aunt Hannah, her only sister living at home, as Annie and Susie were away. Elizabeth could hardly keep track of her two sisters – what live wires they were! They had travelled delivering talks on Ireland all over the USA.

Hannah did not mind. She was part of the children's life and they were part of hers. The minimum upheaval was to be caused to them and when they all went to Switzerland, she would keep house at Grosvenor until they returned. Hannah hoped her sister Elizabeth would return fit and well as she wondered how one person could cope with so much.

The plan was that the children would follow her to Switzerland after her surgery and stay as long as the recuperation took and until she was well enough to travel home. This was the outward story that Elizabeth calmly told her family. She took an active part in all arrangements and pretended it was going to be an adventure. She minimised her illness, and her apprehension of the impending surgery. Within a year of her surgery the rest of her family travelled to Switzerland.

When the Civil War began, Elizabeth knew it would have broken Tomás' heart – Ireland was destroying itself. The concept of divide and conquer once again raised its ugly head. Ireland as a nation was doing its worst to itself. The British government could sit back as the Irish themselves were well down the path of self-destruction. The incredible fact was that brothers took arms against brothers. Fathers fought against sons. It would take generations to repair the damage that this war was going to do.

They lived happily in an area called Davos for almost seven years and when her health improved and she returned from Switzerland in the late 1920s. The house at Grosvenor Place had been kept open by her sisters and she devoted her time to rearing her

children and instilled in them the values and love of tradition that she and her husband had shared.

There was never a doubt that her only son held a special place in her heart. He held the same principles as his father and later fought for a free Ireland.

She admired his fortitude, prayed for him on a daily basis during his long years of solitary confinement. When he walked back into the living room at Grosvenor Place in 1948, she honestly thought that her heart would burst with joy and pride. She had not seen him for eight years. Elizabeth died in 1952, immensely proud of her husband and of her family who were continuing to serve the Republican ideal.

The Children

Siobhán Mac Curtain went on to graduate from University College, Cork and became the first lady barrister in Ireland. She married Noel McNamara, a solicitor. She moved to Strand House in Youghal where she died suddenly in the prime of her life.

> *A rock of courage and common sense*
> *In a sea of utter confusion and horror.*
> *Memories are strange and very mixed*
> *Time seems unimportant yet very real*
> *The truth is always complex*
> *Yet incredibly simple.*

EXTRACT FROM *MEMORIES OF MY MOTHER*

Síle Mac Curtain pursued her love of music and opened a school to teach the harp. Maud Gonne MacBride was a very good friend and when Síle started her career as a teacher Maud presented her with a harp that Yeats had given to her as a birthday gift. It was with great joy and pride that she performed on this special gift. She was part of the Republican movement in the 1940s and led a long and happy life.

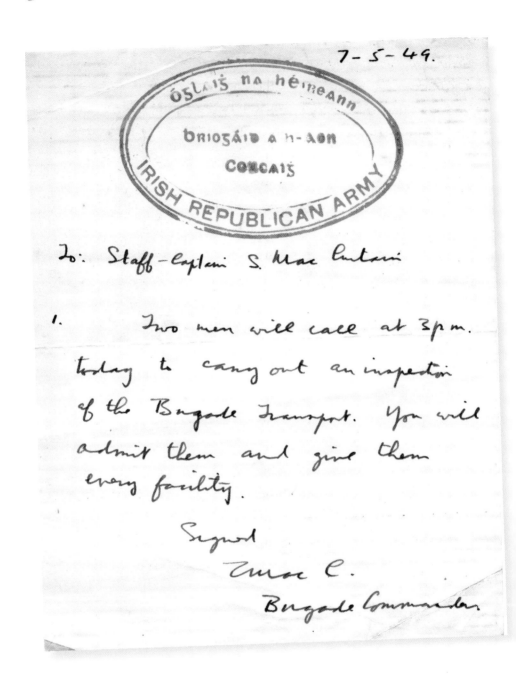

'Two men will call at 3.00 p.m. today to carry out an inspection of the Brigade Transport. You will admit them and give them every facility.' Orders written to Síle by her brother Tomás

Tomás Mac Curtáin referred to here as *Tomás Óg,* followed in the path of his father and his godfather Terence MacSwiney. He walked in their footsteps, but never in their shadow. A marked child, he was harassed throughout his teenage years. Pictured right, wearing his father's Tara brooch, dressed to lead out the Volunteer pipe band.

A Republican by birth he studied intensely and became a Republican by conviction. Tomás served the Republican movement with the same drive and dedication as his forefathers. He became OC of the 1st Cork Brigade and spent his twenty-first birthday on hunger strike and another fifty-six days on a later hunger strike.

Sentenced to death in 1940 by a military tribunal he endured solitary confinement for almost three years and was the first blanket man in Portlaoise jail. Tomás married Mai Furey from The Lough in Cork. The woman, who from first sight was the love of his life, understood him and supported him until his death in 1994. My father was a man of uncompromising principle. I am overwhelmed by the sacrifices that he made and I hope to share his story with you some day.

Tomás married Mai Furey on 24 October 1950, pictured with Dolores Carlton as flower girl

Máire Mac Curtain was educated in Cork and studied medicine at UCC. She married Joe Ward and a number of years later moved to Scotland with her husband and children. Máire was a qualified doctor and had an infectious good humour. She was much loved by all who crossed her path. Her love of Ireland, and more especially Cork, were well known.

Eilís Mac Curtain, the baby in the pram the night her father was murdered in 1920, qualified as a physiotherapist and lived in Dublin for many years. At retirement age, she returned to Cork to care for her sister Síle. Eilís is the sole survivor of Tomás and Elizabeth's children.

Appendix 1

Poem written by Tomás Mac Curtáin to his wife Eilís:

Eilís

Is cuímhin liom, a ghrádh gheal, an chéad uair riamh,
A bhuail um a chéile sinn i Linn Dubh na gcraobh
Thugas searc agus grádh dhuit, is mo chroidhe go hiomlán
A Eilís a' Bhreathnaigh a' chuir m'aigne ar fán.

Chómh deagh-chúmtha cóireach, is camán id' láimh,
Do bheól beag chómh milis, a bhí dom chrádhadh;
Do thabharfainn an uair sin gach a raibh insan stát
Acht go labharfadh Eilís liom go cneasta, modhamháil.

I mí bhreágh na Lúghnasa tháingís im' threó.
Istigh i dtigh Éamainn, cuimhneóchad air go deó,
'Sa tseómra beag gleoite 'n-a mbíodh na ranga ar siúbhal
I Sráid Chumhang an Phínig, a ghrádh geal, mo rún.

Is cuimhim liom do chrot is do chumadh seang caol;
Nuair chuiris do thaobh leis an bhfalla ba shéimh;
Do phreab mo chroidhe ionam is do chailleas mo bhrígh
Go raibh Eilís a' Bhreathnaigh agam-sa mar mhnaoi.

Is 'mó lá breágh gréine chaitheamar araon
Ag siúbhal cois a chéile, ag súgradh 's ag pléidhe
Ba bhocht sinn 'san tsaoghal so acht, ba chuma linn é.
Mar do bhíomair le chéile 's ár muinighin as Dia.

Bhíomair scartha ó chéile leath-bhliadhain nó níos mó,
Bhíos-sa i Luimnigh na laoch im' mhúinteóir
Bhíos uaighneach dubhrónach abhfad ó mo ghrádh,
Is níor chodlas óidhche gan an grádh san dom' chrádhadh.

Níor chóir dom fanúint chómh fada san uait,
Thar n-ais chughat a thánga gan aon phingin ruadh;
Acht bhí dóchas im' chroídhe agus áthas le rádh
Go raibh Eilís i gcomhnuidhe chómh dílis 'n-a grádh.

Shocruigheas m'aigne, chun socruighthe síos
Agus tig deas beag clúthar d'fhagháil dom' Eilís
Chuaidh gach aon rud im' choinnibh acht dhá rud amháin
Níor chaill Dia ná Eilís orm dá ghéire é an cás.

Bhíos ceithre bliadhna fichead is ní rabhas riamh chómh bocht
'Nuair a pósadh i Meitheamh sinn naoi gcéad déag is a hocht;
Má bhíos bocht do réir an tsaoghail níor dhein san mé a
    chrádhadh,
Mar bhí Eilís, mo ghrádh gheal, agam féinig go bráth.

Is anois tar éis ocht mbliana 'nuair fhéachaim-se siar,
Níl aon bhean i nÉirinn chómh dílis léi féin;
Do neartuigh mo ghrá dhi i ngach cruadhtan is cás
Is ag méadughadh a bheidh sé go dtiocfaidh an bás.

Appendix 2

Having told this story, I wish to include the following letter that my father wrote in 1958. It is self-explanatory. It is addressed to Dan Nolan, The Managing Director, *The Kerryman* and refers to the book, *Tomás MacCurtain* by Florence O'Donoghue:

Internment Camp,
The Curragh.
27th July, 1958.

Dear Mr. Nolan,

Now that the serialised story of my father's life has ended in the
"Kerryman", I would like once more to express my appreciation of the
generous gesture of yours in sending me the three copies every week.

The reason I wrote ordering the Cork edition from the "Kerryman"
office was that Eason's could not be sure of having that edition every
week. Now that the story is completed I can get the usual copy here.

If I may, I would like to make one or two comments on the story
itself. First, in the book I think it would be very desirable to have
the Irish text of the diaries, or portions of them, published as they
constitute a very human document and show clearly the heartbreaking
anxiety and disappointment of the leaders in Cork at the turn events
took in the South in 1916.

It had been my intention for some years to edit them myself but I
was restrained by two considerations -

(I) I believe that too many people are talking about their own and
are losing sight of Ireland and

(2) All my time has been given to the task of serving the Cause
for which he died rather than writing about the past. However, in the
first story of his life to be written I honestly think that an effort
should be made to show the qualities he possessed as a writer of Irish.

The other point to which I would like to refer is the fact that
my mother is only mentioned as it were incidentally in the text. In
truth she and my father were completely complementary one to the other
and never did she waver or falter in the help and support and encouragement she gave him in his service to Ireland.

She herself came of Fenian stock and was immensely proud of the
fact, as she was proud that her brother fought with the Citizen Army
in Dublin and "fired the first shot in the Rising."

Naturally I was too young to know or understand anything about
these matters when my father was alive but in the years that followed
we never tired of listening to her telling us of all the men who fought
for Ireland. One of the things she liked to recall was that Captain
Mackey (The Little Captain) used stay in the house at 40 Thomas Davis
Street where we lived, and all down the years as the family was growing
up she continued to teach us that under God our first duty was to Ireland
and that no matter how great the hardship or suffering as long as it was
for the Cause that explained and accounted for everything.

When my father was dying in great pain she said to him, "Cheer up,

2.

Tomas, you are dying for Ireland" – and twenty years later as she said goodbye to me in Mountjoy Prison the night before I was to be hanged she used almost the same words with the same simple finality – "It is all for Ireland." As far as she was concerned there was no need to say more.

Please excuse my volubility but I am sure that I only echo the sentiments of all the family when I say that I would like to see something more of a tribute to her memory in the story of my father's life – because it was her life too – her suffering, her love of Ireland and all that the word "IRELAND" stood for that helped to make Tomas Mac Curtain the man he was.

After his death she continued in the same simple faith and did everything possible to rear her children with a love for everything Irish and to infuse into them the ideal of service to Ireland which was the heritage she got from her Fenian forebears and wanted to pass on to her children.

I hope I have not bored you with this long epistle – which is actually very unusual from me – and I trust you will not take this letter as adverse criticism or anything of the kind.

I would like to thank you sincerely for helping to honour my father's memory – particularly at a time when the 'powers that be' would rather have no mention of the Mac Curtain name and once again for the kind thought of sending me the Cork edition while the story was running.

Yours sincerely,

History tells us Tomás Mac Curtáin was murdered on the 20 March 1920. I hope that I have given a little insight into the man behind the name – the poet, the playwright, family man and soldier. His life achievements were totally overshadowed by his death, but when you hear his name now you might think of him in a different light and understand and appreciate the great passions in his life – God, his country and his family.

I could never do justice to the story of my grandfather and grandmother's life but I hope that by including some of her story I have made up for the omissions in the first book on Tomás Mac Curtáin. My father's wish to include the diaries could not be done in 1958. I am now including some extracts in the following pages.

In the following pages you will find the genuine inner thoughts of a man who devoted his life, short though it may have been, to Ireland, its history, culture and most of all, its struggle for freedom. One must remember that when he wrote these words he had no idea when, if ever, he would be released. Writing was a way of passing the long hours in jail. He never thought that history would remember him and that his actions would be evaluated almost 100 years later.

It is important to note that many of his original writings were taken from him so in various copy books he endeavoured to recall events that were long past, for that reason some of his account of situations are disjointed and past recollections are mingled with his day to day life. They were not written to be scrutinised almost a century later. It should also be noted that it is virtually impossible to translate literally many beautiful expressions and phrases contained in the Irish language. All of his diaries were written in Irish and every day his entry began with Do chum Glóire Dé

Translations [and extracts] from the diaries of Tomás Mac Curtáin:

Tomás Mac Curtáin,
Corcaigh,
Éire.

I was arrested in Cork on the 2nd May. I was put into prison on the Western Road along with ten others; my brother Seán along with them, but we were released again the same evening, because of the efforts of the Lord Mayor and the Bishop and the bargain that was agreed on.

THURSDAY, 11TH MAY: arrested and brought to Detention Barracks, Cork.

MONDAY 22ND MAY: brought to Richmond Barracks in Dublin.

THURSDAY 1ST JUNE: brought to Wakefield in England.

SATURDAY, 10TH JUNE: brought to Fronngach. Tuesday 11th July brought to Reading gaol. Monday 24th July brought to Wormwood Scrubbs for examination by the Advisory Committee, and then back to Reading.

24TH DECEMBER: I was released from Reading and reached home on the 25th Dec. 1916. When I was in prison in Richmond, Dublin I started writing in my diary each day and when it was just full I was brought to Fronngach. My diary was taken from me and it was never given back to me. I wrote from Reading Gaol to the Sec. of State in August and had a reply from him on the 9th September informing me that my diary would not be returned. On the same day one of our friends in London informed us that books and diaries taken from prisoners by the government were being sold in London. An Irishman in London bought one of those books with Cathal Ó Seanáin's name on it. This shows that our books and diaries are being sold and I presume that mine has been sold or lost as well

That is the reason that I am now going to rewrite these notes again as best as I can remember them. There are many things that I cannot remember but there is nothing I can do about that.

Tomás Mac Curtáin
In Reading Gaol
August 1916

Here in Reading Gaol is not the place nor would it be advisable to write the events of Easter Week, therefore it would be unsuitable for me to do so and tell that story. But told it will be at a later date and people will see our side of the story and will see then whether we took the right option or not. Five months have now almost passed and I've gone through many vicissitudes since and I am now of the opinion that we could not have done otherwise than the stand or decision we came to. Some people will say I'm sure that we should have done otherwise but not having all the facts they wouldn't be in a position to make a proper judgement on the matter. The story will be revealed in time and then people will realise that we were not to blame. The Bishop of Cork, Dr Cohalan and the Lord Mayor came to the Volunteer hall in Sheare Street on the night of Easter Monday 'Luan an Éirí Amach' and they told us of the rumours circulating around the city that we were about to start the Rising that night and they came to find the truth of the matter. We replied and told them that there was no truth in the story but that if the police interfered with us we would strongly defend ourselves. They were satisfied with our reply and left. The stories continued in this manner for some days, rumours coming in every hour, day and night and some of our boys [volunteers] furious for action D. Ó Séamus and a couple more – but most of the men were sensible and steadfast and had utter faith in myself and Traolach. They depended on us to make the right decision. On Wednesday a letter came in from Liam Ó Murchu, the Coroner, and Seamus Crosbie saying not to do anything until the Command arrived. The Bishop and the Lord Mayor [Butterfield] came to us again … Both were at the door and having read the letter we let them in. They said the same as the letter and we agreed and they left again. The Bishop and The Lord Mayor came again on Friday and told us they had been speaking to the British army men and that they had said the City was very hostile, and as long as we and the Fianna [Éireann] remained in the hall and they were going to 'Shell' the City if we did not hand over our arms and ammunition. We said straight out that we would not and we also said that the sooner the battle started the better. Then the Bishop said that there were conditions there and that he thinks that the British army meant they would be satisfied if we were satisfied. That is all in the *Free Press* May 20th 1916, and there is no necessity to repeat them here. At the end of that night everything was agreed to except one thing i.e. that our Hall be shut down and the key to be handed over to the Lord Mayor of Cork – these were English Army orders. We said we would not agree to this. We would not close the hall and neither would we give the key of the hall to anyone. The Lord Mayor was of the opinion that the Brits would not be happy with this. We replied that if they were not happy with this refusal, then there would be war. The Lord Mayor returned two hours later accompanied by Captain Dickie and said they were satisfied with these arrangements. It was arranged then that I would go to Limerick and Traolach to Tralee to make similar arrangements there. It was five o' clock when Traolach and myself separated – we had no sleep that night [Friday]. I travelled by train to Limerick at eight o' clock and when I arrived I went to meet our men and speak to them and told them of our arrangements in Cork. They were as badly off as we were. I told them of the arrangement we had made and advised them to do likewise. They did not take our advice and they handed up their arms without any bargaining. Eventually I fell asleep in a Limerick Park, that day I was so tired.

I was back in Cork about nine o' clock and I went to the hall and Capt. Dickie followed on – I heard that some of the men were quite rough with him. Capt. Dickie was trying to arrange to have the arms handed in by Sunday night. We unanimously said that this could not be done. The arrangement made was that nothing would appear in the newspaper about the matter – we put in this stipulation so that our volunteers in the country would not think we had surrendered our arms to the Brits and we had done nothing of the sort and surrendering our arms was the furthest thing from our minds, but that would be what the newspaper would portray or insinuate, and we would not have the opportunity to deny this lie.

The negotiations and bargaining had been done legally, but when we arrived back in Cork on Saturday night, we heard that it was in the 'Constitution' the same day that we had surrendered our arms. We were furious. Sunday morning we went to the Bishop and told him that the arrangements that both sides had agreed on were now broken by the British and neither would we abide by these conditions. The Bishop was frightened. I told him I would not ask the Fianna Éireann to hand over their guns and arms after the Brits had again broken the condition of the agreement – treacherously broken. The Bishop then requested us to allow him to speak to our men and we permitted him to do so.

On Monday night both the Bishop and the Lord Mayor came before the men and after much debate the majority of the men were in favour of putting their arms and guns in the care of the Lord Mayor and that the problem would be put aside for the time being. That was the bargain. We brought in much of our arms that night and that same night the Brits started rounding up Volunteers from the county areas. It was heartbreaking in the following week to see hundreds being brought in. It is often I said to myself that it was an awful pity that I wasn't kept in jail instead of having to watch fine young men, rounded up, handcuffed and being brought in from all parts of the county day in and day out. Towards the weekend, Wednesday, the soldiers arrested the Lord Mayor as well as taking all our guns.

Agreed conditions once more broken, more treachery. I was heartbroken, devastated. Orders were then sent out that anyone in the possession of arms or ammunition were to hand them up immediately.

MONDAY

…. the soldiers searched the city, going from house to house and arrested some volunteers, suspected of having arms. Two of those named Harris and Wickham. All they found in Wickhams' house was a toy gun. After several days of searching the houses in the city they gave up. I forgot to mention that Traolach Mac Suibhne was arrested in Ballinadee (Baile na Dighe) on the 2nd, and was in Gaol in Cork during this period. The Peelers in their searches were always threatening, abusive, bad mannered and even threatened to shoot the women and were very disrespectful. Thursday, about 7.15p.m. the peelers came and arrested me and put me into detention barracks in Cork. I was searched and everything I possessed was taken from me except 'The Imitation of Christ' which I had in English and that little book was a great consolation to me. My wife Eilís gave me a glass of milk before I left the house and so I wasn't hungry. Siobhán my sister-in-law started crying as I was leaving the house but my wife Eilís did not say a word as she did not want to make things any worse for me. (She did not want to make me more worked up than I already was). She told me to have courage and this was a great consolation to me.

I kissed Siobhán, Síle beag and Tomás Óg who was in his cot and then I kissed my wife and went away with the Peelers. I was put in a cell and after all the hassle and worry I felt very tired, without a minute's peace for a month before the Rising. I had no sleep throughout Easter and up to the time I was arrested. I had nothing but trouble and worry and no peace of mind. I put the board (table) on the floor of my cell and fell asleep. I was not too worried being in Gaol myself, as I had been for the weeks previously, as I watched all our young men being brought in as prisoners from around the county by the soldiers and Peelers and I so to speak 'free' in a Cork, oh, and that was the greatest worry and it's often I said during these times I would love to be amongst them and I was almost happy when I was arrested but I would have been overjoyed but for the fact of having to leave my wife, Eilís and the children behind and that was my only worry in this world.

I slept soundly that night. The Gaol bell rang at 6 o'clock in the morning and we got up. Doors were all open at 6.30, soldiers only were in charge of this place and some of them were Irish. Mr O'Donoghue from Friar's Walk was one of them, he had a son who played the fiddle and the bagpipes. I was let out to wash and then I saw that there were a good many of our men here as well. Next to me was Dickeen Fitz [Captain of the Kerry football team] from Killarney. Liam Horgan from the same place, as well as Foley and O'Shea also from Killarney. There was young Hennessy from Cork, Davy Collins from Cork, Tim Reardon from Ballinhassig, Barney O'Driscoll, two Meades – Clonakilty, E. Barrett Kilbrittan, Con Ahern, Dunmanway, Liam Duggan, Dunmanway, Maurice Aherne, Dungourney, Walsh [J.J.'s brother], Donoghue from Ballinadee and Seán Ó hAnnracháin, a brother of Peadar and Tadhg Saor.

At eight o' clock for breakfast I got a mug of some stuff, a mixture of chocolate and coco I think and a piece of bread. As soon as breakfast was eaten a soldier came in the door to me and said, 'have no fear or dread of anyone, but raise your head and look at them all straight in the eye'. That gave me great courage and it lifted my spirits and I did accordingly. It was so and so who spoke to me. (May God bless him wherever he is now.) I will always remember it. We were let out in the air from 11.00 to 12.00 and a guard of soldiers surrounded us. We walked around following one another in line, six feet between each one and we were not allowed to speak. We got dinner which was not too bad and for supper we got the same as we had for breakfast. We had another hour in the fresh air from 4.00 to 5.00. That was how I spent my first day in Gaol. The yard in which we paraded was the one where Tomás Ceannt [may God have mercy on his soul] was executed he was shot a day or two before I was put in.

Saturday was spent just the same as any other day. I asked them for a copy of 'The Imitation of Christ' or something similar in Irish to be given to me but they refused. Sunday was spent in a similar way – almost Mass at 8.00 and when I returned breakfast was brought to me and a few minutes later a soldier ran in to me and placed two boiled eggs in front of me and told me to eat them and that same man did many similar favours for me while I was there and not without danger to himself. He also paid a visit to my wife with news. That was the daily routine up until Wednesday. A little doctor would come in daily to examine us, a nice enough man. On Wednesday Asquith came to Cork. This was the first time the rules were broken. We were allowed to walk and talk at the breaks. I suppose, the men in authority thought Asquith was going to visit the Gaol but he did not come. The odd few were arrested again during the week

Mass on Sunday, and who was there but a brother of Tomás Kent, in the same prison where his brother had been executed. His hand was injured and could be seen with all the cloth bandages wrapped around it and he did not look well at all. That night around 9 o'clock we were notified to be ready for road at 6.00 the next morning. Rumour had it that we were leaving that day so the doctor was to give us a thorough examination.

Morning came; I thought no word had been sent to our families about our departure, but word had been given, for as soon as we were outside the prison gates that morning, the first person I laid my eyes on was my wife Eilís – I don't know who told her. She followed us to the station as we were brought there tied in pairs and the women of Cumann na mBan were there at the station before us in support, but the soldiers would not let them near us. Our lads whistled and sang on our way to the station. We came down Military Hill, through Mayfield Cross and instead of going straight down Summer Hill we turned left at St Luke's Cross near the Church of Ireland and went down Grattan Hill on to the Lower Road and turned right into the Station. Eilís followed us all the way and pretended nothing was the matter and of course she was very worried to say the least. We left the station around 7.30. I have not seen my wife since. We reached Dublin about 12.00 or 1.00 o'clock. The soldiers were very nice and said they were sick of the work they were doing and said they joined the army to fight the Germans and not to fight against their own folk.

We reached Richmond Barracks about 1.30 or 2.00.

We were kept waiting for a long time in the barrack yard. One of the officers in charge of us went to speak to one of the local officers and we were brought into a large hall or gymnasium and given some sort of tack in a large bucket, bread and 'bully' beef. We lay down on the ground and ate it. We were then put into a big barrack room. I was in Barrack Room N1. There were twenty-four in the room and each was given three blankets and were told to sleep on the floor. I forgot to mention that we left the brother of Thomas Kent behind us in Cork, but I heard in a letter that my wife Eilís brought in food and drink for him as long as he was there. This gave me great satisfaction. This was a new type of life altogether for us – there were great crowds of prisoners here. Peadar Ó hAnnracháin, Traolach Mac Suibhne, Austin Stack, Con Collins, Eoin MacNeill, Count Plunkett and thousands of others. There was a plentiful supply of food and drink given to us here. The soldiers in charge of us here were mainly Notts and Derbys, they were hardly able to speak and when they did it was mainly curses and filthy language they used. 'Ten on yer' they would say when accompanying us to the latrines and that was some place, there was no toilet paper there for us. Every second day prisoners were being sent to England. I had two masses there and these were held in the open air, with the soldiers all round with their guns and bayonets. The soldiers would look at us in amazement and at the priest as Mass was going on. I doubt if they had any religion at all ... We had Mass on Sunday and another day during the week. We thought at first that the men from Cork would not be sent to England since we were in a special place near the cook-house, the area known as N.I., but things were not as we thought.

On Wednesday 31, May 1916 we got orders to prepare ourselves to cross the Irish Sea to England. Each of us received a haversack and after three hours of counting and preparation we headed to Kingsbridge Station and crossed the bridge there and down the left bank of the River Liffey. The people gathered and followed, and by the time we reached O'Connell Bridge, thousands gathered around us and they shouted, roared and cursed the soldiers – they were vicious against the soldiers. At last we reached the North Wall. On our way there we noticed the results of the 1916 rising, houses in ruins around O'Connell St. and the Bridge. Bullet marks on all the houses and shops, huge holes in walls done by the heavy artillery – the place in ruins, destroyed as if hit by an earthquake.

We went on board ship at the North Wall and were put in amongst the cattle. I was afraid of getting seasick and I stayed in the air near the hold. Many more came out to where I was so that they could get their last glimpse of Ireland and everyone pretended not to be the least bit worried, but it was easy to see that behind all the banter and humour that they were really worried.

With Éire gone out of sight quietness came over everyone, the good humour and merriment disappeared. Each was thinking when he would be back home or if ever he would. Further trouble awaited as those inside began to get sick, grew paler and paler and were forced to lie down somewhere. There was great silence now and those who were not sick were afraid of their lives of getting sick.

I didn't get sick as the place I was in, out in the air, agreed with me and so I strayed there. It got cold around 12.00 and the cold went through me, but I preferred the cold to the sickness so I stayed where I was. All but a few on the ship were sick. Tom Walsh was on the boat as well and we were both in Richmond together, but when we alighted in Holyhead, Tom was sent to Nuttsford and I was taken to Wakefield. His brother and my wife's brother Jimmy had been in Richmond for a few days but he was brought back to Cork and the Justice gave him two months in prison.

Anyway when we alighted in Holyhead the cold really got to me. We were divided up and myself, Traolach, Peter O'Dwyer and about a hundred more were sent to Wakefield and the rest were sent to Nuttsfield. A train was waiting for us in Holyhead and we left at 1.00 o' clock. We reached Wakefield around ten o' clock. We were tired out after being examined etc., we were brought to our cells at 11. Some of us were in AI which was next to Áilbhe Ó Cadháin, Liam Ó Dugáin, Seán Ó hAnnracháin, Maurice Aherne, Con Aherne, Ed Barrett, etc. it was the worst possible place in the prison. The flagstones in all the cells were wobbly and as old as the hills and were falling apart. Each time you put your foot on one of them a pall of dust would rise from the flags. It was BAD. The first day was bad enough and in the evening I got internal pains and as well as that I had diarrhoea. The coldness of the journey across the Irish Sea, which went through my bones, must have been the cause. I sent for a doctor and asked him to have me removed to the top of the house – Aherne was his name – I heard he was from Cork. He took no interest in me and he gave me some stuff that only made me worse and instead of shifting me to the top of the house he just changed me to the other side of the hall, the same hall. This cell was as bad as the other one but had one advantage. In the first cell you were the last to be served your meals. The food was always cold and the soup would be cold and like dripping. In my new cell I was served first and it was an improvement, even though the food was always bad and if we were depending on these meals solely we would be in a bad state, but we were not depending on the Gaol food. Many people came to visit us and they would bring food, tobacco and such things, and these visitors would include nuns and priests who worked locally. I was unable to eat anything and the internal pains grew worse by the day. I asked one of the two priests who came in if he could bring in a naggin of brandy, having told him of the internal pains and being unable to eat. He said he would do his best. I sent many a letter home that week to the people who used to visit us. A few days later the priest came in and gave me a bottle of brandy and when I went in after his visit I took a few drops and I felt I improved immediately.

On Friday the 9th all the prisoners were called out. And from them a hundred men were called out, including myself, and almost all the men in AI. We were told to get ready to move ... At first I thought we were being sent home, as one of the soldiers told me this, but I had my doubts. Eventually, we learned that we were being sent to Fronngach.

Papers were put before us to sign and we were told that a place was ready for us there in Fronngach in north Wales. I did not like Wakefield one bit, to be sure I was sick while I was there, but apart from that I hated the place. It was thronged with prisoners and we were just about able to go from place to place or should I say from yard to yard. In my opinion it was a miserable dark and unhealthy place. I was delighted leaving the place even though we did not know what was in store for us in Fronngach, all I had in Wakefield was misdirection and misfortune.

We left Wakefield on Saturday morning, 10th June 1916 at 10.00 a.m. and went by train to Fronngach in north Wales. The guards of the Cameron highlanders were all around us and escorted us. These soldiers were pleasant enough and one in particular who accompanied Liam Duggan and myself – Liam was from Dunmanway. We went through Manchester, etc., etc. to Balla and then about four miles to Fronngach. The people in the various stations would look at us in amazement. When we came to Chester one of the station workers enquired of the soldier in command of us and said: 'Irish rebels, isn't it', said he.

'Yes,' said the guard.

'I hear,' said the station man, 'that they are going to rear up again on Monday next,' i.e. Whit Monday. The man in charge did not answer. Eventually we reached Fronngach in the heart of the mountains and it was there that they took from me my note book that I had from the beginning and they would not return it.

Fronngach

We came into Fronngach on Saturday evening at about 6.00 p.m. It is a very small station and when we got off the train we saw the Camp next to the railway just next to us and completely surrounded with barbed wire. We saw the local onlookers walking up and down and each observing from his own patch. These were old soldiers and they were not capable of doing anything and doing that same badly. The Camp was an old distillery once and all the buildings were still there but now changed into one mighty spacious room, higgledy-piggledy style. The Germans were here before us and there were more than a thousand of them and there was not sufficient space for them there in the old buildings.

Since there was not sufficient room in the old buildings timber huts were built outside each holding twenty men. There was a cook house, here, a place for washing clothes and big long rooms for sleeping. There was also a room for drying clothes … we did not put our clothes in there at all. There was a very big dining room. There would be a thousand of us eating there. There

> Tomás Mac Curtáin:
>
> "I only knew him in Fronngach, but had an affection for him there. What a merry, cheerful soul he was. He dearly loved a practical joke. I think I can say without exaggeration that he was among the most popular men in that camp."
>
> Comdt. W.J. Brennan-Whitmore

I THINK I CAN SAY
WITHOUT EXAGGERATION
THAT HE WAS AMONG THE
MOST POPULAR MEN IN
THAT CAMP

was a similar Camp two hundred yards north of our one and that was full of prisoners as well. When both places were full they would hold one thousand eight hundred altogether. All around us were the mountains and some of them were covered with trees. The place was all right during summer, but when the rain came, and often it did, it was terrible. Both Camps were situated well up the mountains. We were surrounded by mountains looking down on the Camps menacingly ...

ALL MAIL TO THE PRISONERS WAS CENSORED

The soldiers were equipped with shotguns and this was very sensible in my opinion because when fired the pellets would scatter in all directions and could do lots of harm, but with a rifle they would have to take aim and this takes time. Many people in Ireland have no time for shotguns and they should have, because they are better and more suitable for certain people than the rifle. The officers' houses are just next to us but on the other side of the barbed wire.

26 July to 4 August 1916

Fifteen of the boys went to Wormwood Scrubbs (Urmwood) today to go before the Advisory Committee ... Art Ó Gríofa (Arthur Griffith), Herbert Pim, Pádraig Ó Máille, Micheal S. Ó Braonáin, Micheál Ó Braonáin, Donnacha … Con Uladh, Seósamh Ó Conghaile, Seán Milroy, Peader Mac Suibhne, Áilbhe Cotton, Éamonn Ó Duibhir, Langley, P. T. Ó Dálaigh, Cathal

Mac Seanáin, Earnán de Blaghad …

I hope they all succeed and that they get the upper hand of the Sasanach, who are trying them. I got a letter from Áine, a lovely long letter, may God reward her. Séamas (Jimmy) is leaving the Cork Gaol on Friday and that is good news. Áine sent some beautiful prayers to me and I am very grateful to her for them. These are the prayers she sent me i nGaeilge, in two forms, one in the form of the Rosary, where for example we would normally say the Our Father, you could say A Chrói ró-naofa Íosa who died for love of us, light up our hearts with love for you. Then on the small beads, where we would normally say the Hail Marys, one could say, A Chrói ró-naofa Íosa, or O Sacred Heart of Jesus, I place all my trust in you.

Áine also said in the letter that the photos that Eilís took last Sunday that I would have them shortly, maybe, that is good news.

The Boys came back from London and Arthur Griffith said to the A.D.C. that they had no authority to question him and that he refused to answer them and he went off. Cathal O'Shannon said the very same thing agus mar an gcéanna le P. Ó Máille agus M. S. Ó Braonáin. They all say that Micheál Ó Braonáin from Roscomáin is going home soon, the first to go and he will be sadly missed as he is a great player on the fiddle. We had a concert tonight and I sang Tír na n-Óg and it was suitable for the time. Yes this is the second anniversary of the Howth Gun Running. It was well done and it is worth commemorating

Every day Tomás meditated on a quotation from *The Imitation of Christ* by Thomas à Kempis. I have highlighted them here in italics.

Sometimes when you want to hear the latest news or up-to-date, you must be ready as well to suffer the resultant worries…

It is a beautiful morning, thanks be to God. These prayers that

SKETCH BY SEÁN MILROY
OF TOMÁS READING HIS
LETTER FROM SIOBHÁN,
TAKEN FROM AUTOGRAPH BOOK

Cell E.3.12 "leitir ó Siobán óg"
Reading Jail

Sean
milroy
15-8-16

Terry MacSweeny

Alf. Cotton

Liam Langley

TOMÁS' FELLOW GUESTS OF THE BRITISH GOVERNMENT IN READING GAOL

I got from Áine are on the wall of my cell in Irish and from now on I will be saying them regularly. Blessed be the Grace of God.

9.00 off to the canteen

12.00. I had a letter just now from Siobhán Óg, which she wrote on the 22nd. In the letter she tells of the story of the fight between Red and Rover and how Red got the better of Rover by cutting his ear and eye. She also had the story about the collision of the two trams on the South Mall, and I suppose damage was done. Also in the letter Siobhán Óg said, 'Mama was screaming all over the house'. What was wrong with Eilís, I wonder. I'll get the truth of the matter later. Well done Siobhán Óg and it (the letter) won't go without thanks from me. When I go home you will get delicacies or dainties from me, dear child of my heart. That letter from Siobhán Óg gave me great joy. I am waiting for the pictures or depending on the pictures every day now and I will be able to see then whether Eilís is in good health or not. I am filling the autograph book bit by bit. I am continually thinking of Eilís. My dearest it is now that I really understand your goodness and your faithfulness and my own great love for you. O dearest (whisper of my heart) what I wouldn't give to be at your side right now at home. But patience, God will put all things right.

Walter Cole

cnt Griffith

P. De Burca

The following is a translation of his effort to compose a love poem for Eilís:

> A thousand loves for ever is she,
> my darling, my dearest,
> above all the women of Ireland,
> like a lamb … well mannered and polite …

He says that the poet's inspiration fails him on this occasion:

> But that does not keep me from saying that my love for Eilís is becoming greater by the day, to such an extent that I will eat her when I go home. Without doubt I will be with her more often than I have been up to now, because she is worth all the care and attention and help that I can give. These are my thoughts here tonight in Reading Gaol and I implore God to keep me in that frame of mind always throughout my life. I thank God for having given me such a wonderful woman and such beautiful children. And with the help of God I will take proper care of them from now on. 'That is my prayer to you O God, that you will watch over them for my sake, that you will keep a very special watch over them for my sake. It is I your servant who speaks to you, who calls you and I am the worst sinner around, but all the same I have the

boldness to ask this request of you. Amen.

Say to the Lord, as the prophet said; Feed me O Lord with the bread of tears and give me to drink in tears generously …

Wherever you are or wherever you go you are an inattentive person if you don't turn to God'. Yes, that is certainly true. No letter came today. I am going to write home now. Yes, but in the afternoon a letter came in Gaeilge from Br Michael in Rochestown and another from Br. Gabriel in the same place.

Br Michael's letter was very long entirely and very good and I am very grateful. Br Gabriel's letter was very good as well. He said he was from Blackpool and was one of the Murphys from Glaisebhuí. Harringtons of Blackpool were relations of his. I cannot remember either himself or his family. I wrote to S … asking her about them. Br Michael sent another letter to me in October but they kept it in London. Br Michael said that Eilís had been down there at a Céilí or something and said he didn't know she had been down until she had left. He said in his letter he was sorry he had missed her but to be sure and come down again … I wrote lots of letters today and I don't know if they'll reach home or not … I use a candle now each night in secret and it is a great help for reading and writing.

It would do us all the good in the world if we were put into a Noviciate again and to teach us good manners, in the hope that it would improve us and be for the benefit of our souls …

Saturday 29th July 1916

It won't be long before you are finished here (in Gaol or in this world). Then see how bright it will be on the other side (outside Gaol or in heaven). A person is here today and gone without account the following day.

It is a beautiful morning, Thank God. I hope the letters go out but I would love to get the photos. Yes, the proofs have just now come. I'm delighted, Eilís is looking great and healthy. May

Toirdhealbhách — mac Suibhne,
" Internment Camp "
Reading Prison,
England. 23. VII. 16.

" Deinid mórán daoine mórán cainnte
agus d'á bhrígh sin, ní cainnt a thír
'n-a gcainnt ach beagán fírinne. "
(L. 3. c. 36)

" Gan saoghal ní gheibhtear suaimhneas.
Gan cath ní bainntear buadh "
(L. 3. c. 19)

(Tomás a Cempis)

Captaen Reading.   Toirdhealbhách mac Suibhne.
Iúl 31. 1916.

TERENCE MacSWINEY QUOTES THOMAS À KEMPIS IN THE AUTOGRAPH BOOK

God keep her. Éamon Sheehan from Cork was here today to see Traolach, Arthur Griffith and Peadar. A girl came in as well, Miss Buckley from Lombardstown, she is teaching here in London somewhere. She took all the letters. I can't for one minute stop from looking at the photos – I'm like a young fellow in love all over again and I would love to be with her every day, but it is wonderful to have the photos, my one desire is to be with her each day. I am grateful to her for having sent me the photos.

May God spare you and your health.

Direct your prayers, your sighs and your tears to God every day, so that your soul will be free when you meet our Saviour on Judgement Day, when you come to die …

On the arrival of Eilís' photo today 'welcome o beautiful picture' because it is you that take the sorrow (fog) or weight off my heart. When I see the face of my wife my one wish is to be sitting by her side. But since it is not possible for me to see my beloved as usual, it is a great consolation to have her photo in front of me every day.

SUNDAY 30TH JULY 1916

In all things remember your last end and how you will stand in the presence of God …
Mass at 9 o'clock – nothing unusual today O'Kelly from London isn't too well in the head today – he is very bad today.

10 o'clock I wrote in Peadar's album today. I am in excellent form today, thanks be to God.

'Test yourself here first and see what you can bear hereafter'.

MONDAY 31ST JULY 1916

Be watchful and earnest in the service of God and frequently ask yourself what brought you in here – or into this world.
That quotation makes a lot of sense and is worth examining more carefully. Everything was as usual today until dinner was over

and then seven men were called out and told they could go home, if you don't mind, and they were Pim, De Loughrey, Piaras Mac Can, Micheál Ó Braonáin (the reader), Liam Ó Briain, Conor Deere, Seosamh Ó Conghaille (Connolly). We were all amazed. I gave letters to Conor Deere to be posted. The whole place was very lonely all that afternoon. About 8.30 that night Kelly got very bad in the head, Jack Bea and he broke the door of the outhouse (toilet) and made an awful racket, the poor man was put into a special room for such people. But friends, this is a sad story for a man who did not mix and who had three lovely children – he was married to a Scots woman and in the letters she wrote to him she reviled him and abused him for trying to be a good Irishman and telling him that she was going to leave him and take the children with her. All this did not do the poor man any good. At the start of the war she exhorted him to join the British army, but he refused and came to Ireland, to Dublin – it is rumoured that he came during Easter Week. But, anyway it is a sad case and may God leave him with a sane mind. This man often complains to me as to why I'm not left go free or let home. But I should be thankful to God that I have my health and a sane mind and I have a good faithful wife at home who would never desert me and who would remain faithful to me always and beautiful children – these are all wonderful gifts from God – even I complain – forgive me Lord in your mercy.

A few minutes ago Peadar Ó hAnnracháin came in to me to chat about the poor man in the padded cell and Peadar finds it very hard to take and has great sympathy for this poor Irishman in our midst. 'O, God free this man and give him his senses and understanding, if you please by your own holy will, a Íosa.'

In the conversation between Peadar and myself about this poor man we had some sympathy as well for his wife. I showed Peadar the photograph of Eilís and told him of the courage and strength I got from her loyalty and patriotism. Peadar looked for quite a while at her photo and praised her. And indeed was I proud and thankful to God for having such an Irish woman for my wife – such a grand fine lady like her, and I deserving the opposite.

All glory to you O Father and I will praise you for ever because

" Nationality is not
a material thing.
It is a spiritual
          thing "

Padraic Mac Piaraic

you have given me such a wonderful wife. Peadar left a bit lonely. There is a cloud over us all here tonight in the land of the Saxon.

Who is the next to leave here?

To be hard on ourselves is the way to spiritual advancement …

TUESDAY 1ST AUGUST 1916

The weather was beautiful today, it was beautiful.

Leave behind youth in this unfortunate world and you will have great peace of mind …

I had a letter from Rose today and it was wonderful. I have one written to her and ready to be sent out.

If you turn away from outside or worldly comforts, you will be able to concentrate on heavenly happiness and you will have comfort and happiness on the inside.

WEDNESDAY 2ND AUGUST 1916

Do not worry who is for you or against you, but be sure that God is with you in all you do …

Nothing unusual today up to 12.00 o'clock.

12.00 D. Mac Con Uladh (McNally) and Doctor … are going home – we were all shocked – we all thought Con Uladh would be the last to be left home. He is to get married in a fortnight – he was very lonesome for the last week with the wedding approaching and he still in prison. Good on you auld Dún na nGall.

4.00 p.m. I wonder who is next to go? We bade them good bye and God bless on their road. I am delighted we met them, as they were men that it was an honour to have known.

ROGER CASEMENT – RÚAIRÍ MAC EASMAINN

Rúairí will be hanged tomorrow morning. He is a generous faithful and loyal man, a real gentleman. What a pity, what a terrible pity.

May God grant you eternal peace Rúairí. I remember well speaking to him in Cork, in the Imperial Hotel – it was a great honour for me. I wouldn't doubt you England for carrying out this dirty deed, but the evil affects of this terrible deed will haunt you till Judgement Day – to the end of your reign and the sooner the better.

I wrote a long letter to Eilís today. The weather is very fine here. We had a drilling or lessons in the Gaeilge this evening and it was very good. Peader was in charge of the lesson.

Never think that thou hast thyself made any progress until thou feel that thou art inferior to all …

THURSDAY 3RD AUGUST 1916

First keep thyself in peace and then shalt thou be able to bring peace to others …

Roger Casement is going to his death now at 9.00 o'clock. May God give eternal peace to his soul. I wonder will they carry it out? Oh, it's a pitiful story and he such a noble and generous gentleman. Kelly was taken to London today and I heard he was put into an asylum

A newspaper arrived this evening and alas it read Casement was hanged this morning. Bad cess to the English for perpetrating such evil, they are the devil incarnate. I am of the opinion that as true as God is above they will pay for it later. His final words from the gallows were, 'I am going to death for my country'. There were three priests in attendance at his execution and he died a Catholic. We were shaking with anger when we read it. Poor Seán T. was crying Rúairí was such a fine noble man – may God have mercy on him, Jesus have mercy on him and may he be seated at the right hand of God.

He who knows best how to endure will possess the greater peace. Such a one is conqueror of himself and lord of the world, the friend of

A mother's love is the sweetest & the best. We only repay in small part that love when we suffer for her. To our mother, Éire, & her martyred sons. And may we, too, be ready for the Call & the Day.

P.T. Daly

Reading Gaol
Aug. 4, 1916.

'A MOTHER'S LOVE IS THE SWEETEST AND THE BEST. WE ONLY REPAY IN SMALL PART THAT LOVE WHEN WE SUFFER FOR HER. TO OUR MOTHER, ÉIRE, AND HER MARTYRED SONS. AND MAY WE, TOO, BE READY FOR THE CALL AND THE DAY.'

Christ and heir to heaven …

A clean mind and a clear conscience, these are the two things that can raise a person above earthly matters …

Today similar to yesterday but again very warm. I hear two new-comers arrived at 9.00 tonight. We had a great debate tonight about the Volunteers.

Joe Robinson and Reader were the two late arrivals in here.

When a person begins to get the upper hand over oneself properly, and progressing in God's way in a manly way, things that at first seem as being difficult and troublesome, would not then bother him any more …

Look for a suitable time to be on your own, for yourself, and often remember God's gifts…

We should not put too much faith in ourselves, because if God's grace

Conptr Gpoven

P.T. Daly

Padpory O1goille

MORE SKETCHES FROM THE AUTOGRAPH BOOK

is missing, then common sense will also be missing ...

The pictures arrived today, two of them. I got three proofs. They are now hanging on the walls of my cell and I love looking at them. I am very grateful to you for having sent them on. It is a great souvenir of the The Rising – true memory. I had a letter from O'Leary as well and so I will write to him and then bed. There is no peace of mind or true joy to be had except in God, the God of glory, God who has no limitations, the God who is in all places.

SUNDAY 6TH AUGUST 1916

To have a clean conscience is the glory of a good man ...

Pádraig Ó Daláigh [Paddy Daly] is going to Ireland on parole and is going to the Trades' Congress. I wrote a letter to Eilís looking for information about May 1st. or was there anything there. Ó Dálaigh was to go around four o'clock but did not go and then he was to go at 8 o'clock and didn't go – he is very lonesome or upset about it. The poor man was very disappointed. We had a concert tonight which was enjoyable. I gave lots of letters to P. Ó Dálaigh to take

with him and a special one for Eilís but I'm afraid now they (letters) won't be going. I'd love if the one for Eilís could have gone, but …
See what manner of man you are in your own heart and take no notice of what others think …

MONDAY 7TH AUGUST 1916

It is wonderful for a person who knows what it means or what it is to love Jesus and who takes no interest in himself for Jesus' sake …

Ó Daláigh did not go as the Governor said he was not to. I didn't get the letters back yet. We washed today – the same as any other day – Peadar gave me a hair cut and gave me a good one. We have a debate to night on Labour and Peader will speak and so will Burke and Joe Robinson.

The person who doesn't look for Jesus does more harm to himself than the whole world could do or even more harm than all his enemies could do …

TUESDAY 8TH AUGUST 1916

When Jesus is present all is well and one sees no difficulties in anything …

I was a steward today – otherwise the day was normal.

We should never get despondent or lose courage. We should unite our will with God's will and suffer all that comes our way in honour of Jesus, because it follows just as the sun comes out after the rain and summer comes after winter and quiet after the storm …

WEDNESDAY 9TH AUGUST 1916

It is not difficult to disregard human consolation [solace] when we have God's consolation …

Nothing unusual today. I had a letter from poor Siobhán.

Your enemies are to your left and to your right and there is no peace to be had from them …

FRIDAY 11TH AUGUST 1916

When out in the yard today, we were called in before the Governor and he told us we had received orders from the government that we were to be kept locked up, as that was the advice given by the Advisory Committee. May God's will be done. I wrote to Eilís telling her all that and also telling her that we were settling down for the Christmas. About a month later I received that letter back and I still have a copy of it somewhere.

SUNDAY 13TH AUGUST 1916

Letters written because Traolach Mac Suibhne's sister coming either today or tomorrow. 10 o'clock and she hasn't come.

MONDAY 14TH AUGUST 1916

The morning is very wet but fine by 12 o'clock.
Áine, Traolach's sister, came today. The letters were given to her and I had a long chat with her.

SATURDAY 19TH AUGUST 1916

I got a pound note today but I wasn't given the letter that I presume was with it. I wrote home acknowledging it. Never got this letter.

TUESDAY 22ND AUGUST 1916

I had a letter from Seán today dated the 15th. and a letter from Minnie dated the 16th. Seán said he was going to pay me a visit. I wrote to him.

WEDNESDAY 23RD AUGUST 1916

A usual day. 'Duke's speech in the paper. We had a meeting as to

P J Doris, "Mayo News" / Westport

Reading Prison / 31st August 1916

Far dearer the grave or the prison / Illum'd by one patriot name / Than the glories of all who have risen / On liberty's ruins to fame.

FAR DEARER THE GRAVE OR THE PRISON / ILLUM'D BY ONE PATRIOT NAME / THAN THE GLORIES OF ALL WHO HAVE RISEN / ON LIBERTY'S RUINS TO FAME

who our leader would be. It was arranged to have an election every month from now on. I have a terrible pain in my head.

FRIDAY 25TH AUGUST 1916

Nothing unusual today, Seán is coming to see me during the next week or so. Traolach is always stuck in his room writing. Seán T's birthday is today. He is going to give a party to the boys – yes we had a great night – eating and drinking with pleasure. Peader Sweeney and myself provided great music.

SATURDAY 26TH AUGUST 1916

I had a letter from Áine, one from Minnie and one from Leo Carroll. I played handball with Art Ó Gríofa (Arthur Griffith) and with Peadar Sweeney. It was a great day. Showers at 4 o'clock. I made an effort to put a cord from MacBride's cell on the top floor in through Figgis' window and then to tie it to something inside and when he'd be sound asleep, the cord would suddenly be pulled and I hoped it would create a terrible racket so as to wake up everybody in the room. But, just as I was arranging the cord in he walked on me and saw what I was up to, but said he wouldn't tell anyone.

SUNDAY 27TH AUGUST 1916

Mass. We played handball in the small yard and I was referee. There was a great game of doubles between O'Connell and Figgis versus MacNiocaill and Sweeney, O'Connell and Figgis won the game. Ó Connaill can be a bit bad tempered.

MONDAY AUGUST 28TH 1916

Handball – wash/shower. Henry Dixon and Doris came from Fronngach to us. Concert, a cake, sugar and tea from home. It looks as if Eilís made the cake.

N. B. A page has been torn out here 29, 30th and 31st missing.

FRIDAY 1ST SEPTEMBER 1916

Earnan [Blythe] is made Commandant today, so Figgis is out of his post today. Malley is treasurer and Áilbhe Ó Cadháin and both of the latter are chiefs and I'm in charge of the wash house. We had a concert, full call for the girls, it was a good night. Seán is coming next week. Monday maybe.

SATURDAY 2ND SEPTEMBER 1916

Life as usual today. No word from Seán. I wonder will he come on Monday. Hubhard is gone on his holidays to Wakefield.

SUNDAY 3RD SEPTEMBER 1916

Mass at 9.00. Spent most of the day playing handball. I wonder will Seán come tomorrow.

MONDAY 4TH SEPTEMBER 1916

Wash house dinner at 12.00.

Seán came about 2.00. He told me that Eilís and the children are all well and that is good news. He gave me a ten shilling note. He was looking great. The letters were given to him. He said his business is going well and I am glad for him.

FRIDAY 8TH SEPTEMBER 1916

Usual type of day. A bed board fell in the hall around 11:00. The man on guard thought Cole shot himself.

SATURDAY 9TH SEPTEMBER 1916

Books came for me today from London. These were the books that Seán brought in with him. They were sent to London to be scrutinised. I was called to Captain Morgan's office and he said that he had a letter from the Home Secretary in London saying that the notes taken from me in Fronngach would not be returned to me. Now I must start all over again and write them as best I can remember them. It is better than never, I suppose.

One of the Boys had a visitor who told him that some Irishman in London bought a book with Cathal Shannon's name on it. That clearly shows that books taken from us are being sold somehow. I suppose my books are sold or lost as well. I got five pounds from Seán Ó Tuama today and Traolach got a similar amount – these monies came from a prisoners fund in Cork. We had a great supper from home and some bacon and we had a great meal. It was a great meal by prison standards. Alf Ó Cadháin had a visit today ...

SUNDAY 10TH SEPTEMBER 1916

It was Alf Ó Cadháin's birthday today and he gave great goodies to us - we had a great night.

WEDNESDAY 13TH SEPTEMBER 1916

Two cakes arrived today from Shandon Street, from Máire I suppose. Everything else was the same.

THURSDAY 14TH SEPTEMBER 1916

Another cake arrived today from the same place. I've been chosen to have a party for the boys here a week from Sunday next i.e. the 24th of the month.

TUESDAY 19TH SEPTEMBER 1916

Siobhán went to Goresbridge.

SUNDAY 24TH SEPTEMBER 1916

My birthday! We had a great night. The guards shook hands with me.

[NOTE: Tomás birthday was in fact on 20 March, he used this date as an excuse to have a party and was delighted that he had fooled the guards into thinking it was a legitimate party.]

FROM 25TH SEPTEMBER TO 1ST OCTOBER

Nothing unusual.

MONDAY 2ND OCTOBER 1916

There are lots of rumours going around these days that a Committee or something of that sort is to be set up to put us on trial.

SATURDAY 7TH OCTOBER 1916

I had a letter from Eilís.

About 10.00 last night or early this morning I had a dream. Eilís and myself were in a house somewhere. There were lots of people there. Eilís left early and I followed her. She was in bed when I arrived and I joined her. I kissed Tomás and then Eilís and she seemed extremely happy ...

MONDAY 9TH OCTOBER 1916

Nothing unusual except that there is talk about peace. I am of the opinion that I won't be allowed home before Christmas but be patient. In bed at 10.00 p.m.

TUESDAY 10TH OCTOBER 1916

Yesterday I smoked too much and felt terrible sick entirely from 5.00 until 8.00 and I felt OK again then. I had two dreams that night – the first one I thought I was coming in to Dublin Street Blackpool and then came to Mullane – the cobbler's house. I had a newspaper in my hand and there was some article in it written about me regarding some case that was to come before the court and I was telling him that I didn't understand what it was all about. Then he was telling me that a summons had been sent out that would make me appear before the court. The next thing was that Seán and myself were at the door of the house, No. 40.

Someone opened the door and Susie Walsh was inside brushing the floor of the shop and there was a cloud of dust all over the place and all around her. The next thing was there in the kitchen was myself Seán and Eilís all together. Seán then asked me to rescue the man in the garden behind the house and to bring him in. I said I would do so on the following day, but Seán said that it might be too wet the following day. Then Seán himself went out to take him in. The next thing was, that there I was, myself, herself and Tomás Óg in the bed in the bedroom. I kissed Tomás and herself hundreds of times. Just then I woke up with her and we had more of the same as we had the last time. Then we thought we heard someone coming up the stairs, both of us got up and we saw someone standing next to the bed, beside the window, with a long plait of hair down his back and then I saw his features and his face was very dark [scowl]. He was dressed in a man's clothes I think.

From 11 October until 28 October there was nothing out of the ordinary except one comment 'I have received no letter from Eilís recently …'

SUNDAY 29TH OCTOBER 1916

I heard there was a terrible storm in Cork.

SUNDAY 30TH OCTOBER 1916

Things arriving in for Halloween.

TUESDAY 31ST OCTOBER 1916

We had a great night, all kinds of food and drink apples, nuts, rings, buttons and bits of wood in the cakes, that were brought in to us. A great night. It was unanimously agreed that I was to be leader [chief for the next month] I did not want the job but I had no option but to accept it.

WEDNESDAY 1ST NOVEMBER 1916

On Friday I was accepted as leader Commandant.

THURSDAY 2ND NOVEMBER 1916

Mass and communion. Six came from Fronngach …

SATURDAY 4TH NOVEMBER 1916

Word from Josie saying that Tomás was sick, but that he is improving again. God bless them.

MONDAY 20TH NOVEMBER 1916

There was much talk about peace and us going home.
Peadar Sweeney sang:
I can do what I like with my old mike

All the week from Monday

He's making as you please with … of bread and cheese

But he likes a bit of meat on Sunday …

SATURDAY 25TH NOVEMBER 1916

Mac Cumhaill went home three weeks ago for a week and hasn't come back yet. Éamon Morcan went and his time was up yesterday. He hasn't returned. Proinsias T. Ó Dálaigh went on parole today. I don't expect to be home for Christmas. The other day a flood burst in on them in Blackpool and I have no account yet of the amount of damage done.

9.30 p.m. Eamonn has come back just now. P. T. Ó Dálaigh went on parole and he came back after a week.

MONDAY 4TH DECEMBER 1916

Éamon Ó Duibhir (O'Dwyer) went about a week ago to see his sick father, but word came yesterday that his father had died and is buried by now, I suppose, I'm not sure whether he was in time or not. The War goes on as usual and the Germans are making progress.

Seán Ó hAnnracháin sent me a letter about two weeks ago and he's being kept in London.

THURSDAY 21ST DECEMBER 1916

Duke's speech in the 'Tigh' Duke of Well, in Parliament.

FRIDAY 22ND DECEMBER 1916

It is in the papers today that the Duke said to Parliament that they are shortly to release all the prisoners. Thanks be to God.

A telegram came from Alf Byrne saying that the orders were out and we were to be released. Thanks be to God.

Eilís

Is cuimhin liom,
a grádh geal

When I was a prisoner in Richmond, Dublin, I began
to put down notes in a book every day and I had it just
filled when I was taken to Frongoch.   The book was taken
from me there and I have not got it back since - I
wrote from Reading (Jail) to the Secretary of State
asking him for it, in August, I received an answer from
him on the 9th day of September saying that it would not
be given to me.

The same day we got news from a person who was visiting
one of the boys that books were being sold in London
which the Government had taken from the prisoners and that
R.J. Ryan, Irishman who was there bought one of them and
Cathal O'Shannon's name was on it.   This shows that our
books are being sold by the Government and it is my
opinion that my note book is either sold or lost as well.
That is the reason why I am going to rewrite the notes as
well as I can remember.

There are lots of things which I will not remember
but there is no remedy for that.

                    Tomas Mac Curtain,

                    In Reading Jail,

                    August 1916

Cunntas Cinnlae Tomás Mac Curtáin
a scríí sé i mbliadhain 1916.

(Leanamhaint)

Bealtaine 11adh (Diardaoin) timpeal
7.15 um tráthnóna táinig na póiléirí
airís agus gabhadh mé - cuireadh isteach
sa detention barracks mé i gCorcaigh
- Cuardeadh mé agus tógadh uaim
gar aon rud a bhí agam ac
amháin "Airís an Chrois" a bhí agam
i mbéarla, leabairín ana bheag ab'eadh
é; agus ba mhór an sólás dom
é - cuireadh isteac sa cell mé.
Tug Cit's mo bean gloine.bainne
dom sar ar fágas an tigh agus
ní raibh aon ocras orm. Tosnuig
Liobán Drisinn mo céile ag gol nuair
abhíos ag fágaint an tige ac ní
dubhairt Cit's mo bean focal - níor
mhair leí aon buairt a chuir

orm níos mó ná bí orm ceana
agus bí sí á rád liom muna i beidh
agam. ba mór an cabair an méid
sin dom. pósas Siobán agus Síle
agus Tomás óg a bí sa chabáin
agus annsan pósas mó bean
agus imigeas i dtreanra na
bpiléar. Sead, cuiread eu cell mé
mar a dubairt ceana - agus raréis
na h-oibre t-o téir bíos ruaseai
go léir ní raib puinn iúncais
agam le rí roinus an Cinuje Amai
rí raib aon codlu agam aimsear
an Cásga geall leis, agus suas
go drí an lú rózad mé ní raib orm
aé buair agus rublóid agus cráidgeair
i eagas an bórd ar iúrtár mo
cella agus iuiéas an codla - ní
raib morán buaira orm bei

sa Corcaig. Bíos ar fad na
seachtaine roimhe ag féachaint
ar na (m)buachaillí agus iad ag teacht
isteach ón gClondae ina bpríosúnaigh
ag na saighdiúirí agus na píléirí agus
mise a bhí orra go léir, mar a d'fhéachfá
saor i gCorcaigh. Ó b'sin é an buairt
ar fad, is minic a dubhairt i rith na
h-aimsire sin gur breág liom
bheith 'na measg agus bí áthas
orm, geall leis nuair a tógadh
mé. Béadh áthas ar fad orm
gan amhras acht aniar mo bhean
C.I.s agus na leanbaí beaga
bheith im' dhiaidh nó raibh aon
trioblóid eile orm sa domhan.
Codalaeas go maith an oidhche sin.
Bhíead clog ar a sé achtog ar
maidin (dea Haoine) agus éirigheam

Do oscaladh mo dhoras agus na
dóirse go léir ag 6.30, Saighdiúirí
ar fad a bhí i bhfeidil na háite seo
Éireannaig cuid acu - Mac Uí
Danacada ceann aca ó Lasán
na mBrácar - bí mac age na
~~byca~~ beirtideoir agus 'na piobaire
teogad amac mé cun mé féin do
nige annsan coxnac go raibh
ana cuid eile de's na buacaillí
su carcar im'reamra.
bí inaire liom Dickeen Fitz-
(Capzaon luir umreaza líaxroide
Ciaraide) - ó * C. Háixne
liam na h Arzán ón áur céadna
Foley - ón áur céadna
Ó Seaġda ón áur céadna
Young Hennessy - Cork.
Davy Collins - Cork.

Jim Rearden - B'hassig .
Barney Driscoll
2 meades - Clonakilty
E. Barnet - Kilbrittain
Con Ahern - D'way .
Liam Duggan - D'waaper.
Maurine Ahern' D'gowney .
Walsh (J.J's brother)
Donoghue - Ballenadee .
Seán Ua hAnnracáin - Driúer Do peadar
Tadg Saor.

[tá cuid den learanon glán annsan - is dóca
go raib sé cun ainmneaca eile a cuar
síos nuair a cuimnigead' sé orra).

Tugad dom muga ~~srup~~ srup éigin
ar a loir actog agus píosa aráin
meascad chocolate agus cocoa abead
ain deoc is dóig leam.

Díreaċ nuair a bí an breuġeas sin
tite aġam ráinig saiġdiúr an doras
isteaċ euġam aġus ar seisean—"Ná
bíoḋ eaġla ort—na scár roim aoinne
anso" ar seisean " air árduiġ do ċeann
aġus feiċ orra ġo léir" ar seisean "
idir an dá śúil". Ṫug san misneaċ
ḋom aġus ċuir sé spreoḋ ionam aġus
deirniġ amlaiḋ.—
Dṫar an ċainṫ sin liom (ġo ġcuaiḋ
dia an rái air pé air'ṅa bḟuil
sé anois) (Cuimneóċaḋ ar sin ġo
bráṫ. leoġaḋ amaċ pé'n aer sinn
ġo léir ó 11 ġo na ctoġ aġus ġárda
saiġdiúirí mór-ṫimpeal oraimn
bímis aġ siubal mór ṫimpeal
indiaiḋ a ċeile—ṫimpal té ṫaoiṫ
óna ċéile aġus ni leoġṫaí ḋúinn
foral do ráḋ te ceile—Kuair amaċ

dinnéar ná raib ró olc ar fad
agus an rud céadna a fuaramar
ar maidin a bí againn arís mar
súipéir um thráthnóna. bí uair
a cluig eile féin ar againn
ó ceathair go cúig a chlog.
Sin mar a caitheas an céad lá
sa carcar sin. Sa tslíg na
bímis ag eubhal do eukead. Tomás
Ceann (go ndeanaidh Dia trócaire
ar a anam) tar éis é tánaic - tá
nú do sar ar eukead. sreaic mé
do mharbhujead Tomás -
Dia Sairdaidhn caitheas ar anzcum
céadna. D'iaras orra leabaic
mar "duixis an Crúish" ingaoluinn
do rabaire dom ai ní rabarfaí
Caitheas an Domnaí ar an zcum
zicéadna zeall leis - Aifreann

timpeal a hoir. Nuair a tánaig zar
nais bí an breugfear curría isteac
cugam agus cúpla néomar na
diaid' rir saigdiúr isteac cugam
agus leog sé ar an gclár os mo cómair
dá ní beirigire agus dubairt
sé liom iod d'ire. Din an fear san
ceadna rudaí beaga dom an
faid a bíos ann agus ní gan
conrabairt do féin a din sé
é. Cuaid sé cun mo mna le
sgéal cúpla uair. bí mar sin
go dtí Dia Ceadaoin gan aon
airiú. Tiocfad Doirúirín beag
isteac zar ná ag áromúcad
firín deas go leór —
Dia Ceadaoin ráinig Asquitte
go Corcaig. Sin é an lá ráinig
an céad brisead ar na

Riaghalacaib teigad dúinn casur
le céile agus siubal i dtreannra
céile mór timpal. Ceap lucir
smúcria na háire go raib Asquith
ag teacir ag rialladsria is dóiġ
liom air níor cáinig — rugad pó-
dúine isteac aon draiar i rit na
seairmaine sin — cáinig an
Dominic — Cuadamair go h-Áixream
Cé bí ann aic dríbíar do Tómás
Ceannr — sa prísún ceadna inar
marbuigead a drbíar — bí a lámi
gonruije — bí balcaisí éadaig
pille uimir agus bí sés ag géúciam
go holc.
An oidie sin timpal a naosacloig
rugad pósra dúinn beir ollam
i gcóir an bóiair ar maidin
arasé, bí an pápla mór

timpal go rabamair ag maireán
i rith an lae agus dein an doiteán
sgrúdú pé leir orainn.

Tháinig an maidin — Ceapas ná
beadh aon eolas ag ár múinteir
ar an oireú' ai ambasa, bí, mar
mhair cúas ar a dtaob amuic de
dtigeora an príosún ar maidin
bé an céad duine teogas mo
shúil air ná é. Is réin, mo béan.
Ní feadar cé mas dí é.

Lean sí go dtí an stáisiún agus
sinn ceangailte le na céile agus bí
mná Cumann na mban ag an stáisiún
roimeann ai ní teogfad na saigdiuiri
in aur linn rad — bí na buacaillí
ag amhrán agus ag feaduigheal ón
bpríosún go dtí an stáisiún.

Thánamar aníos Cnoc Mililtory treaska

go Croisire na mbóir agus in lonad
reair síos díreac 'Cnoc an t Samraid.
D'iompuigeamar ar clé ag croisire
na mbóire inaac an teampaill gallda
atá ann agus síos chor garrain
a tánamar agus amac ar an
mbóthar Toirearaic. Lean Eilis sinn
anslige ar rad agus níor leog
sí urrir go raib aon buacar
urrir - D'fágamar an stáisiún
umpeal 7.30 agus amac tinn
ar siubal go baile átá Cliat.
Ní faca mo bean ó soin —
Scroiseamar baile átá Cliat
umpol a dó déag nó ah-aon - bí na
saigdiuirí ana-deas agus bíodar
á rád go rabadar bréan dén
obair atá to déanam acu.
Gur cuadar san arm cun troda

déanaṁ i gcoinniḃ na ṅGeáɾmáiṅ
agus ní cun sroda i gcoinniḃ a
muinntir péin — scroiseamar
Barracks Richmond umpal 1·30
nó 2 a clog de ḋéaṁ, Aibreán 22. 1916.
ḃíomar ag ṗeiṫeaṁ
isteaṁ sa ċlóg mór ar ḟead 'zamall
ṁaiṫ; ċuaiḋ an toiṗizeaċ a ḃí os
ár zcoṁn ċun cainte le oipizeaċaiḃ
na háite agus ar ball cuiread ar
cúbaḋ airíṡ sinn agus cuiread
isteaċ sinn. Halla mór ~~~~
mar ḃeaḋ gymnasium abeaḋ ann
[Sporndann]
ṫugaḋ roinnt zae d'úinn i mbuicéad
mór, asan, agus "bully maer ṗeóla"
luiṫeamar síos ar an ḋtalaṁ,
agus ċaiṫeamar é. Cuiread isteaċ
ansan sinn i ngarleann de na
ṡeómraiḃ móra — Barracks Rooms.

Ní I an ceann na rabas — bí ceitre
duine fúid ann rugad. Trí blaincéidí
do gac duine againn agus d'órduigead
dúinn codtu a déanam ar an ralam
ar an gcuma san. D'earamadar te rád
gur fágamar Mor Uí Ceatur in ár
ndiaid .g Corcaig. Airigeas na diad su
gur tug Eilís mo bean biad agus
deoi isreai dó an fiad a bí se
ann agus bí árias mór orm
mar geall air.

Saogal nua ar fad a bí san
áit seo. Bí na sluaigte príosúnaigte
ann — bí Peadar Ua hAnracáin
ann agus Tadolas Mor Suibine,
Austin Stack, Con Collins — Eoin
Mac Néill, Count Plunkett
agus na sluaigte nár iad
bí fluxe bid agus dige tabarta

anso.

Notts. and Derbys a bí a bfurmór des na saigdiúrí a bí i bfeaḋt na háite — Do b'iongantaċ na fir iad — fir beoga salaċa, iad go tiuġ agus is beag an méad caimnce a bíodar ábalta ráḋ aċ eascaint agus droiċcainnte i gcomnuiḋe. Teu au yeu a bíoḋ aca a ráḋ Annuacra a bídís ag ár dtionntacáin go dtí an laiġeir ag do b'iongantaċ an áir féin é sin. Ní bíoḋ puinn luimeacaira ann agaunn. Gar fé tá biod eud des na prisunijie á ġeur go Easana — bí dá Aifreann agam ann — agus amaċ fé'n speir a bí sé agaunn agus na saigdiúrí mór timpeal orainn le na ngunnaí agus a bagnenrí. Biod' na saigdiúrí

ag féacaint orainn agus iongnad
orrtha agus ag an sagart nuair a biod
an tAifreann aige á rádh ní raibh
aon chreideamh in aon chor acu san,
is dóigh liom.

Bhí Aifreann againn ar an
nDomhnach agus bhí lá saoire idir na
seirmeacha.

Bhíomar ag cuimhneamh i dtosach ná
cuirfí go Sasana an dream a tháinig
ó Chorcaigh mar cuireadh i dtír féin
sinn, un Seomra W I in ar ug
an Chócaireacht ar ní mar a síltear
abhíorr agus.—
Dia Chéadaoin 31/5/1916. Fuaramar órdú
sinn féin d'ollamhú i gcóir na
bfairrge um dul go Sasana
tugadh iabhrsach do gach duine
againn agus tar éis irihuire

chug ar Cómairleam agus a socrú
fé deire ghluaiseamair amac as an
áit síos go Kingsbridge trasna na h-abann
ansan agus síos fan na h-ábann ar
an draoib clé. bailiġ na daoine mór
timpal orainn sa tslíġe agus sar ar
scrioseamair Droicead Uí Conaill bí na
sluaiġṫe ag búiriġ agus ag béiciġ agus
ag easgainí ar na saiġdiúirí - bíodar
go fíocmar i gcoinnib na saiġdiúirí
fé deire sxrioseamair an North Wall.
ar dul ann dúnn connac riamn na
rioda mór timpal Droicead Uí Conaill
na tiġre go léir leaġṫa, rian na
bpiléar ar gac tiġ mór timpal agus
pollaí móra ar na fallaib ná raib
tr'éis ruzimós na plaoscaib - mór
a cur na gunnaí móra isteac
orra bí an áit go léir rabta

scr aċ ṗe mar a béaḋ sé. Dá mba
luaṡgaḋ ṡalman aṫṫ ann.
Cuaḋamair ar an mbáḋ- Cuireaḋ
measc na imbe ṡreac ann - bí eagal
ormsa roim breóṫreaċir naṗuinṫz
agus ḋ'ṗanas amaċ ṗén aer in
aice an ḣold. bí ana-ċuid des na
buacaillṫ amuiċ san áur ———— sin
ṡṫréó a's goḃṗeuṗ.ḋís ṡalaiṫ na
hÉireann - go mbeaḋ Raḋair
deireonnaċ aca - bíoḋar go léir
ag teoẓainz orṫa má naiḃ aon
buaicir orṫa aċ b'ṗuiṫiṡze ḋ'airinz
oriaṗṗé aunẓreann go rabadar
buaḋaria go teor.
ḋ'ṗáẓamair Éire mar ndiaḋ agus
muair bí sí imiṫiẓire as ár Raḋair
ẓáinẓ cuiṁeas orainn go léiċ agus
ḋ'imiẓ an ẓreann agus an imeiḋreaċir

bí gac duine ag muirnani ar
cúram a íocfad' sé íar nais ~~nós~~
nó a íuocfad' sé íarnais in aoncor.
ba zeaRR zur ráinzr zRioblóid eile
aRann d'éiriz na daoine a bí iszig
ón aeR ana bréoize indiaid' ar
indiaid.

        Srad an zkó ezrus an cairt
Cipeá duine ezrus f éaiaurz zriobloideac
az reair na súiib - a azaird az ~~baine~~
baineac; sleamnóc sé iszeac in ár
éizur ezrus luidfead' sé síos - ba zeaRR
zo Raib ana - ciúineac sa lóng - ana
cuid daoine bréóize ezrus na daoine
ná Raib - eazla an báis orra. Roims
an bréóizreacra. Mí rabas bréóize
ezrus nuair a fuarras amac zo
Raib an áir 'na rabas féin an aeR
az réidriú cóm mair san liom níor

coṡuiẟeas as. Bí an oiḋċe ana ḟuar
ẕimpal a ḋó ḋéaẕ aẕus bí an ḟuaċt
aẕ ḋul ẕríom aċt b'ḟearra ḋom an
ḟuaċt ná an ḃreóṫreaċt aẕus ḋá
ḃríẕ sin ḋ'ḟanas maṫ a ḋíos. (Robard?)
Ẕimpal ḣeaṫ-uaṫ bí ẕaċ aoinne
ḃreáṫ sa lonẕ aẕus ẕaċ ḟví ḋuine
bí Ṫomás ḃrearnaċ ar an lonẕ leis
bí se i Richmond im ẕeanẕa air ṁuaṫ
a ṫánamaṫ iDír i Holyhead cuṫread
Ṫomás ẕo Wuttsford aẕus mise ẕo
Wakefield. Bí a ḋríṫar (aẕus ḋeiraṫ mo
ṁoċeile) Seamus i Richmond leis air
ḟeoḋ'cuṫta tá air ruẕaḋ'ẕaṫ mas
ẕo ḃarcaiẕ é aẕus inẕ na ruíẕaiṫí
[ní ḟeaḋar cad é an ḟocal é sin — magistrate
is ḋóċa ṁí ḣuḋmar sin] aṫsan ḋá
uí sa ḟrísún do.⁺
Ḟe ḋeire ṫánamaṫ iDír

aẕus de ḃáṟṟ an ṫá uí ṟan bí ealaẕ aʋé aṫ an ḃṟṟṟaṫ
ṟimẕ ḋo bí na healaẕ ẕá ḃ́ṟeiḋ ḃáẕ ann ẕaʋd ʋa ḋiuḋ ẕi
bí ḟuṫ ṁáḃ́ a ṫiuṫẕ im ʋáẕ ṟṟẕ a ṫṟẕ ḟeaʋ ḋ́em áʟuṫé
ḋá ṫ́ṟṟṟuṫaṫ

bí an fuar ag goil go cruaidh orm
deineadh roinn(?) orainn ansan
cuireadh mise, Riala(?), Peadar, Ó Ua
Dubir agus ana cuid eile rumpal
céad ar Rad go "Páirc a' Toraim" (Wakefield)
agus an cuid eile go Mullsford
bí traen ag feireain linn ag
Holyhead. Gluais an traen rumpal
a haon agus scroiseamar "Páirce
a' Toraim" rumpal a deic a clog
bíomar ana iunseaċ, tareis
scrudú a déanamiorainn agus
rudaí den tsórd sin bí a haondeag
buailte sar ar cuireadh sa cell
sinn. Isteaċ san AI a cuireadh
cuid againn. Bí im aice, Ailbe Ua
Caḋain, Liam Ua Dubġain, Seán
Ua h Annraċáin, Maurice Aherne
Con Aherne Ed Barret 7c. 7c.

MERCIER PRESS
WHAT YOU NEED TO READ

MERCIER PRESS
Douglas Village, Cork
www.mercierpress.ie

Trade enquiries to CMD Distribution
55A Spruce Avenue, Stillorgan Industrial Park, Blackrock, County Dublin

© Fionnuala Mac Curtain 2006

ISBN: 978 1 85635 573 5

10 9 8 7 6 5 4 3 2 1

A CIP record for this title is available from the British Library

Mercier Press receives financial assistance from the Arts Council/
An Chomhairle Ealaíon

Printed and bound in the EU